Sshhh...Calm your Anxiety...

A Step-By-Step Guide to Facing Life's Challenges, Learn to handle situations and Accept Yourself.

Table of Contents

Introduction

Chapter 1 Face Any Anxious Situation You've Been Avoiding

Chapter 2 Put an End to Anxious or Intrusive Thoughts

Chapter 3 Learn Mindfulness Skills to Cope With Depression-Related Challenges—One Deep, Cleansing Breath at A Time

Chapter 4 Discover Words of Encouragement as You Build the Confidence, Self-Acceptance, and Clarity You Need In Order To Break Free Of Depression-Related Thought Patterns and Create Lasting Change

Chapter 5 Filled With Warm Affirmations

Conclusion

Introduction
So...you're living with anxiety?

You might be reluctant to admit it. You might stick to the script of "I'm totally fine!" despite thoughts in the back of your mind saying otherwise.

If, on the other hand, you have struggled with anxiety for a long time or just recently found out about it, then I urge you to keep reading. Don't worry; I won't leave any subtlety out this time around as I'll open up and share my personal story and struggle with anxiety right here on the first page. No skimming required :)

You see, everyone experiences anxiety in their life to some degree. It's an innate human emotion that has kept us safe for thousands of years.

But for some people, like myself, anxiety doesn't go away after an exam or a stressful day at work. Anxiety becomes an unfortunate part of the everyday routine and can often be debilitating.

In my case, it all started in late 2012 when I began experiencing intense panic attacks during exams or even while doing homework. The attacks were irrational and totally out of my control as I felt light-headed and anxious beyond belief. I thought nothing of it since this was "normal" for everyone, right? Well...not exactly.

It was right after my first semester in college that I realized that something was going on. I reached out to my mom and asked her if she had ever experienced anxiety symptoms as she has been an educator for more than 20 years. I don't recall the exact conversation we had but the outcome was surprising to me even now.

She told me she felt there wasn't anything wrong with me, but that this was "just the way life is". I proceeded to have a complete meltdown as it really bothered me that adults (who are supposed to know) can make so many mistakes when it comes to helping teenagers.

The next day I started to do some research on anxiety and realized that it is in no way normal for a 20-year-old to feel panic attacks or feel stressed constantly. I wasn't at the point where I needed help from a doctor so I decided to see what my friends thought about this (after all, "everyone" was feeling this way, right?).

I casually asked them if they had experienced any symptoms (lightheadedness, fatigue, etc.) and was bewildered as all of them said no. This was when I realized that something was seriously wrong with me.

I went online and searched "anxiety symptoms" and was surprised by the amount of information I found.

I was truly astonished by the sudden flood of resources all in one place! It seemed silly to think that this wasn't something that people should know about. After all, it had been prevalent throughout my life thus far!

As I read more about anxiety and consulted friends and family though, I began to realize that many realized something was going on but they didn't understand it or get help for it until later in life (e.g., college).

At the time I was also dealing with a lot of changes at home. We had just entered college and my parents were quite busy with that. I wasn't sure what was happening with me but I knew something was wrong as it was affecting me greatly.

I had been having trouble sleeping, felt very low most of the time, and had lost a significant number of friends and family members (which could be due to the fact that they left my school).

As my mom approached me one night to say goodnight, she asked me if I could tell her anything about myself. I wasn't able to. I was unsure of what was going on and didn't want to worry her, even though I knew she would be concerned if she knew what was happening.

After talking to my mom, I realized it might have been my anxiety that had caused me not to want to tell her anything about myself. (I felt like my anxiety had brought a part of myself out of the closet and put it in a dark room).

I started learning more about the signs and symptoms of anxiety and depression, as well as the best ways to manage them. Doing this helped me to understand why my mental health was an issue. I was able to recognize that I had been struggling with my own symptoms of anxiety and depression for years.

Using the insights from reading more about them, I became better at managing them. I realized that my negative self-beliefs weren't true and that there were things that could be done to help manage them.

After being diagnosed with anxiety, depression, OCD, and PTSD, I began seeing a therapist who knew how to best help me. He helped me identify what triggers were causing some of my negative self-beliefs and what thoughts were contributing to those triggers.

Through the combined expertise of my therapist and my mother, I was better able to understand and manage my symptoms of anxiety. As I monitored what was happening, I was able to recognize situations in my life that triggered anxiety and recognize if I was being overly anxious during those times.

Understanding how much control I had over it helped me to become more aware of the consequences of an overemotional reaction.

I then learned about the proper medication that would help me with my triggers and negative self-beliefs. It wasn't easy at first, as suddenly I had to take pills every day that would make me feel drugged and lethargic. But again, by monitoring how these effects were affecting me on a daily basis (e.g., lethargy, drugged feeling, etc.), I was able to realize that these negative effects were actually helping me. As I felt the effects of my medication (e.g., less anxiety, clearer mind), I realized that the reasons I had anxiety in the first place were the same symptoms I was trying to get rid of. For example: less anxiety meant less negative self-beliefs. Less drugged feeling meant a more clear head and better thinking about life situations and not just what's going on in your head/mind.

Learning how much control I had over my symptoms helped me cope with them and become more aware of how they affected me.

Through the help of my therapist and my medication, I have been able to recognize what situations caused me to become anxious. Because of this awareness, I know that if I go into a situation where anxiety is likely to be triggered (e.g., talking to new people about topics/subjects that may make me feel embarrassed/dreadful), I will feel severe symptoms approaching.

I now know how to manage these symptoms before they get out of control and manifest into a panic attack or feeling extremely depressed and emotional about issues. As an example: If I go into a situation where anxiety is likely to cause me distress, but don't notice any symptoms approaching (e.g. when riding on the subway) I will simply take a deep breath and remind myself that it's anxiety and take a step back from my negative thoughts.

I know now that these thoughts are only thoughts, they aren't reality. I also know that I have control over the way I feel about myself and my ability to do the things I want to do. Knowing this has helped me become more emotionally resilient in challenging life situations where stress arises.

The biggest change that's happened for me since being on medication is that I've been able to recognize how anxiety can manifest in different ways. I'm no longer afraid of what my anxiety will manifest itself into. I'm more aware that anxiety can cause me to have racing thoughts and feel like I've lost control (even though I know I haven't).

For example, when the subway stopped on my way home and started to fill up with people, I felt an intense amount of drugged-like symptoms coming on. My first response was to become very afraid. For some reason, it was the first time that this had happened. After I realized what was going on (a panic attack), all that was running through my mind were thoughts of feeling trapped/like something bad would happen. I had to remind myself over and over that I wasn't trapped and there was nothing wrong. Even though it seemed like I was, I knew there was nothing actually wrong with me.

I told myself over and over: It's anxiety, not a life-threatening/dangerous situation. It's okay to have panic attacks but they're not painful physically or mentally. I'm safe (even though it felt unsafe).

When I realized the thoughts in my head were all about fear, they simply changed from being an uncomfortable feeling to something more manageable. I was able to learn to stay calm and have my mind clear. I could think about what I was going to do when I got home instead of thinking about how I felt.

While it may not seem like much, this helped me overcome the fear and panic attacks that had occurred. After this experience, I never experienced another one of those feelings again on the subway train.

After being on medication for a few months, my mental health began to stabilize. I'm still learning ways to improve my mental health (e.g., more exercise). But awareness has helped me become more resilient in challenging situations and become more emotionally intelligent (better at dealing with life's challenges).

Awareness has helped me cope with my anxiety and recognize the difference between something real and something in my head. It helped me realize that I have control over my negative self-beliefs/thoughts and learn to be more aware of the way they affect me.

When I was first diagnosed, there were things I didn't understand about my anxiety. Awareness has helped me deal with them better by understanding what's happening to help myself before they cause distress.

The awareness has also helped me become more aware of what's going on when I feel anxious or depressed so I can recognize the pattern as early as possible (i.e., I'm feeling anxious, I'm feeling negative about myself, etc.) and have some control over what's happening. Being able to recognize what's happening helps me learn how to deal with the triggers (e.g., what causes me to feel anxious?).

I now know how to manage symptoms before they get out of control and cause me serious distress. For example: During a panic attack when I was riding on the subway I began to get afraid that something bad was going to happen (i.e., something bad will happen on the train or that I'm trapped because it came to a stop). I had to remind myself that I was safe, there was nothing wrong with me, and anxiety can make my thoughts turn to the worst possible outcome.

Awareness has helped me realize that I have control over when anxiety starts to occur and what things trigger it. Even though I can't control when they happen, I know that if things don't go well (e.g., a friend will hang out with them without inviting me), my anxiety or panic attacks will be triggered.

This is definitely a heavily personal thing, but as far as recognizing the difference between real-life threats and imagined problems, awareness has helped me grow into a better person since being diagnosed with social anxiety disorder.

When I first realized I was diagnosed with social anxiety disorder, I began to look it up online. Reading other people's experiences (especially people my age) really helped me feel more comfortable with the fact that I had a mental disorder.

I also began to look at social anxiety/social phobia as being responsible for things that happened in my past (i.e., why didn't they invite me to their birthday party? They must've not liked me because of my social anxiety...). This caused me to become very depressed and negative about myself.

Awareness has helped in this area by allowing me to recognize and change the way I view what happened in my past. I now understand that these things happened because of a mental disorder and I have the power to control my emotions and how I feel about myself.

As a whole, awareness has helped me recognize and deal with all aspects of my social anxiety. It has also helped me become more emotionally resilient in challenging situations.

Awareness has helped me accept myself as a person living with social anxiety disorder. It has made me realize that even though I have a mental disorder, it doesn't define who I am as a person or what kind of person I am (e.g., I'm still innocent, not a bad person or untrustworthy).

Awareness has helped me realize that my social anxiety is something I can control. It doesn't have to be something that controls me.

Awareness has helped me accept the fact that no matter how hard I try, I will feel anxious and have symptoms of social anxiety disorder. But it's also helped me realize that when I don't try, they can get worse and even make me feel out of control.

Awareness has made me realize the importance of being open when it comes to talking about mental health (e.g., coming out about having mental health or mental health awareness). It has taught me that it's okay to admit when I feel down or I'm worried about something.

Awareness has helped me learn how to deal with the symptoms of social anxiety disorder. For example, I learned that when I feel anxious in a group situation, the best thing for me to do is remind myself that it's okay to be nervous and negative thoughts will turn into negative feelings if I'm sitting there worrying about what other people are thinking about my appearance or my social interactions.

It has also helped me learn how to deal with situations where people are tense and don't want to be bothered by me because they're insecure/negative toward themselves (e.g. an acquaintance asking me to hang out/texting me a lot, etc.).

Overall, awareness has helped me realize that although I have a mental disorder, it's not something I can't control. It's something I can learn how to deal with and live with. It's made me more confident in my abilities as a person and realize that I'm not the only person who experiences these symptoms.

Awareness has helped me become more aware of how my thoughts and feelings affect my body language when I'm meeting new people or talking to someone new, for example. This will help me realize if my anxiety triggers are getting out of control before it gets too bad (e.g., panicking).

Awareness has helped me realize that I'm capable of being in a situation where I feel anxious or uncomfortable. It taught me that it's okay to notice and accept when I feel nervous, negative thoughts coming into my head, etc. and that it's okay to not be perfect all the time and make mistakes (e.g., expressing interest in someone, saying something awkward, etc.).

Awareness has also helped me realize how my self-consciousness/negative thoughts can affect how much I like myself. Knowing this will help me be more aware of when these feelings are getting out of control (e.g., feeling negative about other people's opinions or myself).

Awareness has helped me accept and understand that even though a lot of people have told me that I'm not perfect and that I need to learn how to be more open, a lot of people also have told me how pretty I am.

Awareness has helped me realize just how easily other people can judge or become jealous of others who are confident, outgoing, etc. It has taught me to learn from these experiences so I don't make the same mistakes or get too negative about myself.

Overall, awareness has helped me understand that even though I have a mental disorder and it's something that impacts my daily life, it's not something that can change the way I speak or interact with others.

Awareness has helped me realize that I can control how I feel and how confident I am.

And my favorite part - awareness has made me realize that coming out and living with social anxiety disorder is okay!

Long story short, awareness has changed the way I see myself and my identity as a person. It has helped me begin accepting not only my mental health as a whole, but also the fact that even though I have a mental disorder, it's not something that controls who or what type of person I am.

I know for some people, social anxiety doesn't have anything to do with mental health or psychology. For them, it's just an issue they're going through and they'll eventually get over it. But for me, having social anxiety disorder and understanding the way it makes me feel has taught me how to live with it and control it. It's also taught me the importance of having awareness in other aspects of my life.

Awareness has made it easier for me to handle situations where I feel nervous or uncomfortable because I know that by acknowledging my feelings, thoughts and body language, I'll be able to deal with them better.

It has also helped me become confident in my abilities as a person by teaching me that even though I have a mental disorder, it's something that can't change who I am or how I approach a situation.

Awareness has helped me realize that even though I have a mental disorder, it's okay to still be me.

Think of anxiety as a high-pressure surge on a garden hose. The pressure the hose creates is designed to clean your driveway efficiently; but if you are standing in front of it, it's going to blow you away. Every day, we all experience some sort of anxiety — which can feel like mild neediness or acute terror — but only some people learn how to deal with it effectively, and others continue suffering.

This type of anxiety is characterized by persistent worrying thoughts and feelings that just won't quit. In most cases, GAD sufferers feel anxious all the time rather than just occasionally. They're convinced that something terrible will happen, and their minds go into a high-gear overdrive to prepare themselves for it.

In order to understand GAD, you have to understand the different components of the condition. There are two types of anxiety, according to Dr. Abasolo: social anxiety and situational anxiety. Social anxiety occurs when we're around other people and uncomfortable situations; situational anxiety involves us feeling uneasy when we're in various kinds of situations we don't expect to be in – like public speaking or going grocery shopping.

But in order to explain how it works, we have to first put the pieces of the puzzle together.

Types of Anxiety and the Brain

When you're anxious or fearful about something, your body language gets tighter and you might hold your breath or hold your stomach. The physiological response is designed to help you either get away from the danger that's troubling you, or prepare yourself for any worst-case scenario. We do this because our survival depends on it: we need to fend off against threats, hunt food and escape from predators. Our brain plays a big part in making those physical responses happen, but let's look at the neurochemical behind anxiety first.

The part of your brain that makes sure you're ready for a fight is called the amygdala. It's often called "the emotional brain" because it can play such an important role in our lives. The amygdala gives us emotions like fear and anger. But the amygdala also expresses emotions we don't notice when we're in the heat of action: like sadness and anxiety. They are common to all mammals, as well as to other primates like monkeys and humans and birds. We've seen them portrayed on TV shows, where they're usually referred to as "guts."

When the amygdala is activated, we experience intense fear and anxiety. The neural pathways in the brain that were meant to convey rapid information over short distances—like a scream for help—are routed to areas where we feel emotion. As a result, our brains allow us to experience emotions like fear and anxiety over longer distances; just because they're not perceivable by touch or sound doesn't mean they don't exist. This is a good thing because it means that if a dangerous animal jumps out at us and we don't hear or see it, there's still a chance of survival, because our body will remember the pattern of movements that might have alerted us to danger.

This makes the amygdala a powerful diagnostic tool in diagnosing mental illness. Compulsive disorders, for example, are disruptions in how your brain reacts to stimuli. So what happens when you have a fear of germs? It's normal to feel anxious around them, but when you compulsively wash your hands or use bleach or other cleaning products, it could mean that your brain is being overactivated by the fear of germs.

There's no greater feeling than speaking from the heart. Here are some tips, tricks, and habits to try to help you overcome that nagging feeling of anxiety.

1. Take a deep breath and remind yourself that your mind is playing tricks on you and overreacting to situations.   2. Write down what's worrying you or giving you anxiety

about what's been going on and use it as a reference point for when your anxiety starts coming up again in the future so that you can remember that it doesn't need to be this bad and just needs some time to work itself out like with any other problem

3. When you feel anxiety coming up, give your mind something else to focus on. Your mind can't think about two things at once so if you give it something else to think about like other activities or people that bring you joy, you'll find that the anxiety goes away and doesn't come back.

4. Take a walk and listen to some music or read a book. Music is great because it's pleasing and distracting but doesn't require too much effort to fixate your attention on

5. If it's really bothering you, write a letter to the person causing you anxiety and put it where you can see it every once in a while (you don't want to make them feel guilty)

6. Try to avoid using your phone when you're feeling anxious for at least an hour or two. Use a landline instead and focus on

talking with your family or friends. Remember that

7. If things seem out of control, just stop and calm down for a while but then pick up where you left off after.

Chapter 1 Face Any Anxious Situation You've Been Avoiding

We all have anxiety in different situations, and it's completely normal! But sometimes it can be easy to overthink those worries and become overwhelmed by them. But here are 7 ways to face your anxious thoughts, no matter how big they seem.

#1 Return to your senses- Ground yourself in the present by focusing on what you see, hear, taste, smell or feel right now. This way you'll know that at least one thing is real in any situation.

#2 Accept uncertainty- In order to get past our fear of uncertainty we have to realize that there are many different paths we can take and every path has unlimited potential outcomes. For example, if you don't know what the future holds, then you can never be sure of a single outcome! If you live with uncertainty expect to feel anxious when these feelings come up.

#3 Try your hardest- If you cannot harness the power of your anxiety to focus your mind on something positive try trying to do your hardest. The more honest and alive we are when we are doing our best, the more we will likely excel.

#4 Let go- Focusing on the anxiety that arises in situations is counterproductive and only serves to magnify it. So try letting go of emotion and physically removing yourself from situations that make you anxious. Sometimes it is helpful to keep busy while in situations that make you anxious.

#5 Accept something bad- The worst thing you can do is accept negative outcomes or events as 'good'. You might say, "It's good that I got fired because it will teach me a lesson. I'm sure I learned something from it." But actually, you're just saying it over and over again because you've learned that this is what people expect. Appreciating the negative can lead to poor self-perception.

#6 Focus on your thoughts- This is so important! When you focus too much on a negative event you can give it more power than it deserves. For example, if someone talks negatively about your job do not automatically assume that they are right just because they said something negative about you. Listen to what they said and try to understand their perspective.

#7 Tell yourself the whole truth- Be honest about the feelings and reactions that you have to events. Are you worried about something? Do you feel anxious or mad? Accept these feelings and tell yourself that they are normal reactions to a certain situation. This will help you become more comfortable with your emotions and help you handle situations in a better, healthier way.

#8 Identify triggers- Do something that makes you feel uncomfortable or stressed out even if it's small. Over time, these experiences will be able to grow from stressful but manageable into stressful yet manageable.

#9 Repeat the process- Keep repeating the process and always remember that you are in control. Feelings of anxiety will never go away but you can learn to be comfortable with them. By identifying your triggers, repeating this process, and learning to understand what makes you anxious you will eventually be able to overcome your anxieties one step at a time!

#10 Understand that most of these anxieties are positive- Anxiety is a sign that something is wrong and that you need to change something in the way you look at things. It shows that there is a passion inside of you. It's good to be anxious about everything because it means there's more at stake for us rather than just going through the motions every day.

It is natural to feel nervous before or after a worry-inducing event. But anxiety disorder, also known as generalized anxiety disorder, is defined as chronic and excessive worry that can't be controlled. The severity of the condition varies from person to person, but it often causes debilitating stress and emotional instability.

We will walk you through some practical tips for beating GAD by acknowledging anxious feelings and trusting your instincts.

GAD is a serious mental illness that can have long-lasting effects on both your physical and mental well-being. And if you or someone you love is suffering from this condition, it's critical that you get the help you need.

The Trouble with Worry

When an anxious thought comes to mind, it can be hard to shake. So why does worry persist? The answer lies in how our nervous system functions. Neurobiologists have identified several parts of the brain that are activated when worries emerge in conditions like GAD. These areas are responsible for generating anxiety and negative emotions such as worry, stress and fear.

When a person is in a threatening situation, the limbic system, amygdala and hippocampus process that information. The limbic system, also known as the emotional brain or primitive brain, produces fear by passing on messages from the amygdala to the hypothalamus. The amygdala sends out chemicals like adrenaline to your heart in order for it to beat faster and pump more blood to your muscles so that you can run away when you sense danger.

On the other hand, your hippocampus functions to make sure that you associate something with the situation that caused it so that you don't get stuck in a loop of nervousness. The part of your brain called the frontal cortex weighs your options before you decide what response is appropriate.

When your amygdalae and hippocampi process fear-inducing information, they produce another chemical, called cortisol that activates your sympathetic nervous system. The sympathetic nervous system reacts with the pituitary gland so that it releases adrenaline into your bloodstream. This prolongs the fight or flight response in the body.

If you become physically aroused during anxiety, you are more likely to have symptoms after the fact because of this prolonged release of cortisol. This could include sweating, rapid heart rate and shallow breathing. However, if you stay calm during an anxious moment, you are less likely to experience these symptoms afterward.

However, even though your sympathetic nervous system tries to calm you down, it can't do the job on its own. So your brain kicks in and tries to reduce the amount of cortisol that is pumped into your body. That's why people with GAD often experience stress-induced insomnia or feel disoriented and achy after an anxiety attack.

Although all of these symptoms could be explained by stress hormones, it's not always easy for us to separate them from the anxious content of our thoughts. Since our brains are more concerned with reducing those cortisol levels, it may seem like we have simply made things worse for ourselves when we worry about high-stakes situations in our lives.

That's why our brains appear to be making our lives worse when it comes to dealing with anxiety. However, all of these symptoms could be explained by stress hormones. Cortisol is released into your bloodstream during the first few minutes following an anxiety attack as a way to calm you down and make it more difficult for you to have another one in the future.

This is why people with GAD often experience stress-induced insomnia or feel disoriented and achy after an anxiety attack. However, it's not always easy for us to separate these symptoms from the anxious content of our thoughts. In fact, our brains are more concerned with making us feel bad about those cortisol levels than they are with reducing those cortisol levels. That's why anxiety symptoms can sometimes seem to make a problem worse when you have them.

To get a better sense of how we experience anxiety, consider the following experiment.

Three people reach into their pockets and pull out exactly the same amount of money—$5. However, each person believes that they had a different amount of money in their pocket before they pulled t out. Although all three people believe that their $5 is exactly the same, the difference in how those $5 make them feel has a huge impact on their behavior and emotions afterward.

For example, lady #1 might spend her money on a quick snack, assuming that she had $5 in her pocket. She had only just enjoyed a full meal, after all. Lady #2 has the $5 in her pocket but does not feel confident that that is the same amount of money that she put into it before pulling it out—she is anxious about spending the new money on something frivolous. Therefore, lady #3 might withhold some of the $5 and put it back into her pocket for safekeeping. Lady #3 fears that if she spends all of the $5 on a quick snack, there will be less money for paying off debt or getting something special for herself when she gets home.

These three women have three very different experiences of $5 and anxiety.

CDC: GAD Statistics in America

If you suffer from GAD, you undoubtedly understand how significant this condition is for individuals, their families and their coworkers. The U.S. Center for Disease Control (CDC) has been producing a detailed report about GAD in America since 2008—and the statistics are impressive. The most recent 24-month data from 2015 indicates that approximately 8 million adults in the United States have Generalized Anxiety Disorder (GAD). An estimated 1 in 8 adults (13 percent) will experience a period of generalized anxiety disorder over the course of a year.

More than half of all adults with GAD (58 percent) have not been diagnosed with the disorder. Of those who have sought treatment for their GAD, only one-fifth (21 percent) seek help from a professional. Only about onequarter experience significant improvement after treatment.

There are many risk factors that increase the likelihood that you or someone you love will develop GAD. Those factors include:

Being female. Women are much more likely than men to suffer from GAD. This is because women on average experience more stressful life events than men and tend to internalize their stress. For example, women are more likely to be stay-at-home parents, they are more likely to care for aging parents and they're also more likely to experience dietrelated health problems—all things that increase your risk of developing anxety disorders.

Women are much more likely than men to suffer from GAD. This is because women on average experience more stressful life events than men and tend to internalize their stress. For example, women are more likely to be stay-at-home parents, they are more likely to care for aging parents and they're also more likely to experience diet-related health problems—all things that increase your risk of developing anxiety disorders. Having a stressful event or history of trauma. People who have been through a traumatic life event in the past are at a significantly higher risk of developing GAD. If you have experienced a major loss or trauma in your life, you're at an increased risk of all anxiety disorders.

People who have been through a traumatic life event in the past are at a significantly higher risk of developing GAD. If you have experienced a major loss or trauma in your life, you're at an increased risk of all anxiety disorders. Having a history of mental health problems. Research indicates that experiences with depression, alcohol or drug abuse and other mental health problems make it much more likely that you will develop an anxiety disorder.

Research indicates that experiences with depression, alcohol or drug abuse and other mental health problems make it much more likely that you will develop an anxiety disorder. Being male. Men are generally less affected by stressors than women, which contributes to their decreased risk for GAD as well.

Men are generally less affected by stressors than women, which contributes to their decreased risk for GAD as well. Being younger. Research shows that people who are younger than 25 or older than 55 are at lower risk for anxiety disorders. However, you should not assume that you won't develop an anxiety disorder as you get older. For men, the risk of developing an anxiety disorder increases by age 30 and then reaches a plateau after age 43—meaning that no matter how old you get, it's never too late to make changes to reduce your symptoms and prevent further problems.

Research shows that people who are younger than 25 or older than 55 are at lower risk for anxiety disorders. However, you should not assume that you won't develop an anxiety disorder as you get older. For men, the risk of developing an anxiety disorder increases by age 30 and then reaches a plateau after age 43—meaning that no matter how old you get, it's never too late to make changes to reduce your symptoms and prevent further problems. Having a family history or genetic condition. Anxiety disorders in children may be related to a family history of anxiety or other psychiatric disorders in their parents.

Anxiety is an incredibly common problem that can affect anyone—even if they thought they were pretty bulletproof before they got the diagnosis. When you live with GAD, you're likely to feel isolated and alone. That means that you're more likely to develop anxious behaviors that can lead to even more problems down the road.

What Are the Symptoms of GAD?

To stay on top of your anxiety and manage it properly, it's important to understand what the most common symptoms are for your specific disorder. If you have GAD, these are the signs that appear on the outside—the ones people might notice without receiving a diagnosis from a doctor.

Physical symptoms

Stomachache. Anxiety disorders are characterized by physical symptoms, including: nausea (you feel sick to your stomach) aches and pains in muscles, back and joints shortness of breath or trouble breathing or swallowing When anxiety occurs on a frequent basis, such as every day, these physical symptoms can become worse. If you're experiencing any of these physical symptoms regularly—and it's interfering with your ability to function on a daily basis—it's important to make an appointment with your doctor so that they can determine whether or not you have a case of GAD. Pounding heart. Your heart rate may be faster than normal in response to stress, which can cause palpitations (rapid, irregular heartbeat) and make you feel lightheaded. Chest pain. You might get chest pain when you breathe deeply, or when you stand up quickly. Sweating. Sweating is a common physical side effect of anxiety disorders that can affect everything from your appearance to your ability to work through the day. It's important to remember that these symptoms are not evidence that you have an anxiety disorder; they're simply an indication that your body is getting ready for action because something is on its way. Dizziness or lightheadedness. This is a common physical symptom of anxiety that frequently affects people with panic disorder. It can make it hard to carry on with your regular activities. Mental and emotional symptoms

Feeling anxious or tense. When you have an anxiety disorder, you might feel tense all the time, even if you're not in a stressful situation or it's not an ordinary time of day for you to feel this way. You might feel like your body is always ready for danger and is looking for problems that aren't there. Feeling jumpy or easily startled. You might be startled by loud noises and sudden movements that would otherwise be easy to handle. That leads to feeling jumpy, which might cause you to constantly second-guess yourself and start worrying about things that have nothing to do with your current situation. Being overwhelmed by everyday obligations. You might feel like you have too many things on your plate, or that you're always behind on everything. You might feel that the world could suddenly end at any moment—and this can be incredibly painful and overwhelming as it happens, but doesn't help when you're experiencing it. Feeling useless or hopeless. With panic disorder, this symptom refers specifically to the sudden severe feelings of panic and fear; however, with GAD, all types of anxiety can leave you feeling anxious and hopeless about the future. Cognitive symptoms

Not recognizing your situation. Unless someone with an anxiety disorder is deliberately hiding his or her symptoms, you'll notice that people who struggle with anxiety have trouble recognizing what's happening to them. This is because they might be so used to the physical and mental effects of the disorder that they feel like they have no control over it at all. Feeling scattered mentally. You might experience a lack of concentration, forgetfulness or problems with memory (or you might notice this as an occasional symptom, but not as a regular part of your life). Staying focused on one thing for too long can make it difficult for you to keep up with unrelated things, which can then leave you feeling confused and lost in the moment. Thinking too much. Having too many thoughts going through your head is common for people with anxiety. This can leave you overwhelmed by the constant chatter that's happening in your mind. It may even seem like it's a separate entity, since thoughts might make you feel offkilter, like something is changing in your brain.

How Are Anxiety Disorders Treated?

Treatments for anxiety disorders can vary depending on where you live, who you see and what type of anxiety disorder you have. The most common treatments for GAD involve a combination of different types of therapy and medications prescribed by your doctor who specializes in affective disorders.

Cognitive Behaviors Therapy (CBT)

CBT is one of the first things that people with anxiety disorders will be recommended. CBT is often prescribed for GAD, although there are other types of therapies that might provide some help. By practicing CBT, you can learn a few skills and coping mechanisms to help you manage your anxiety without letting it take over your life. This therapy focuses on helping you recognize what causes your anxiety and teaches you how to change the way that you think about the problems in your life.

This type of therapy focuses on four main areas: cognitive restructuring, exposure therapy, relaxation exercises and lifestyle changes.

Cognitive restructuring involves identifying negative patterns of thinking and replacing them with positive thoughts. For example, you might start with the thought that being in a public place gives you anxiety; instead, you can recognize that this is untrue and work to change it to "being in a public place doesn't give me butterflies, but just being outside is okay because I like the air." exposure therapy involves learning how to handle situations that give you anxiety. For instance, you might learn breathing techniques to keep yourself calm when placed in an uncomfortable situation. This can be helpful when your anxiety is so strong that your body feels on fire and your heart is racing out of control. Relaxation exercises are a great way to calm yourself down when your body is feeling on fire. These exercises involve deep breathing and relaxation responses that can be practiced while you're lying down or thinking about calm things.

Finally, lifestyle changes are another form of therapy that people with GAD should consider. These changes can help you not only overcome your anxiety, but also enjoy life more because you'll have a better understanding of what gives you anxiety and how to handle it. Maybe you can replace the bad habits (like overeating) that often cause your anxiety in the first place with healthier habits (like eating healthier foods or taking up exercise). Or you can start thinking more positively by replacing negative thoughts with positive ones.

Medications for anxiety disorders vary depending on the type of anxiety disorder you have, but some medications are commonly used to treat the symptoms of a panic attack. The most common types include antidepressants, which are commonly prescribed in combination with CBT; benzodiazepines, which are mood-stabilizing medications and often prescribed in conjunction with antidepressants (to help reduce the severity of panic attacks); and beta-blockers, which calm down the nervous system.

Antidepressants for anxiety disorders are commonly prescribed to people with GAD. They can help you feel more at ease by reducing the intensity of your anxiety, while possibly working to reduce the number of panic attacks that you have.

Benzodiazepines for anxiety are also commonly used to treat anxiety. These medications work to calm you down by working on your nervous system and helping to regulate the levels of the stress hormones adrenaline and cortisol in your body. They are often prescribed in conjunction with antidepressants and used when you start having panic attacks, during which the medication works as a fast-acting sedative to help keep your heart rate and blood pressure steady.

Beta-blockers are typically used to calm your heart rate and regulate the levels of adrenaline and cortisol in your body. They can help you relax when your anxiety has you on edge, while also helping to reduce the severity of panic attacks.

How can I find a therapist?

If you think that you might be struggling with an anxiety disorder, it's a good idea to seek support from a mental health professional. Not only can they help you learn more about the types of therapies that work best for you, but they can also help you overcome the symptoms of anxiety and learn coping mechanisms that make it easier for you to handle situations that make your anxiety flareup.

If you're in the United States and you need help finding a therapist, there are many different ways that you can do this. You can:

There are therapists located all over the United States who specialize in treating anxiety disorders, but also across the world. If you live in an area outside of the United States, you'll have to contact your local mental health professional for assistance finding someone who can help treat your symptoms of anxiety.

Contact your local mental health professional or visit your local community college to find information about therapists who are trained in treating anxiety disorders.

Speak to your primary care physician about your anxiety and see if they can refer you to a therapist.

What's the best way to avoid getting anxiety?

The first step in avoiding anxiety is highly debatable. Most people with an anxiety disorder say that it stems from a difficult life experience, like losing a loved one, being bullied or suffering from depression. That's why it's so important to practice mindfulness techniques and use relaxation responses at times when you start feeling overwhelmed by life.

People who treat their anxiety with medication report that they preferred anti-anxiety medications because they provide a quick fix and feel more effective than counseling.

If you can't find a therapist, you might also try learning from people with an anxiety disorder. If you find someone who is willing to talk to you about their experiences, it can help to understand what causes your anxiety and how it affects your life.

If you're interested in learning more about how to overcome your anxiety without medication, or if your doctor is hesitant for any reason to suggest a particular treatment, there are many options available for treating GAD that are both affordable and effective.

For example, you could consider trying cognitive behavioral therapy, which involves learning to identify negative patterns of thinking that cause you to feel anxious. You can also work with a therapist to learn more about the types of treatments that have been proven to be most effective, such as exposure therapy.

The good news is that no matter how severe your anxiety is, there's always a better option for treating it than self-medicating with medication. If your anxiety is keeping you from living the life you want and feeling more at ease in social situations, talk to your doctor or mental health professional about finding help sooner rather than later. Together, get the care and treatment you deserve.

Chapter 2 Put an End to Anxious or Intrusive Thoughts

Do you find yourself shaken by intrusive and anxious thoughts? Do they constantly trouble you, no matter what you do? You are not alone.

Anxiety is a monster that many people live with but never tell anyone about. It can be hard to talk about or ask for help with anxiety because there is often no visible cause and it can come out of nowhere at any time. But the good news is that anxiety is manageable! There are so many ways to take charge of your life and put an end to these troubling thoughts, including starting here...

Anxiety

Anxiety is a tricky beast. It comes out of nowhere and it won't go away until you do something about it. It can strike almost anyone, and it will often come in waves from time to time. And the unfortunate truth is that anxiety doesn't discriminate between people: no one is completely immune to anxiety attacks. You might have had an anxiety attack once or twice before, but if you've never had one, don't be fooled into thinking that they are rare - like nightmares or getting a toothache, they're just as common but less well-known. And like toothaches or nightmares, anxiety can be pretty scary when it happens for the first time!

But why do people experience anxiety? Are we all just overthinking things and getting worked up about nothing? The answer is no, the physical symptoms that are an integral part of anxiety are your body's way of reacting to a perceived threat. If you suffer from anxiety then deep down you know that there is something more to these intrusive thoughts than just a run-of-the-mill overthinking session; they just feel different and seem to have a life of their own.

Luckily for us, there are some simple techniques that can help you to realize that you're not really threatened and put an end to those intrusive thoughts once and for all. Get Support

Anxiety doesn't just strike everyone; it is something that often affects people who have lived with their problems for years. You don't have to suffer in silence because you have been living with anxiety for months or even years - it's a good idea to seek support from others in order to know that you're not alone. An anxiety support group is a great place to start your search for help. If your anxiety is still too strong for you to attend one, you can always contact your GP and ask for a referral to join a self-help group.

A few members and a great atmosphere make all the difference to many people. There are also online self-help groups if you prefer an online space to meet people.

The most important thing that you can do is trust your instincts, which come as part of the problem and not as a solution. It's really hard to be in charge of yourself when these intrusive thoughts continue tormenting you every day; the best thing that you can do is find someone who will give you some advice on how best to deal with anxiety once and for all.

Realize It Isn't You

It can be scary when you lose all sense of control over your own mind, but you may want to try and look at this from a different perspective. It's not really that your thoughts are just going around in circles, it is more that they are being kept alive by a constant stream of negativity. If you could let the negative flow continue then it would end up being out of control. The key thing to realize about intrusive thoughts is that they will continue as long as you keep them alive in your head by sticking with those negative feelings; it's like they are feeding on those feelings of fear and worry.

You can really help yourself at this stage by thinking about all of those bad things that you keep worrying about. Ask yourself if they are honestly that likely to happen, and then think about whether there is any way that you could stop them from happening if they did. If the answer is no, you could try to distance yourself from those feelings by knowing in your head that these things are unlikely to happen. This can really help you if you start to get overwhelmed by the thoughts.

Stop thinking about bad things

If like me, these negative thoughts are making it hard to focus on anything else, then you can use the thought-stopping technique I mentioned earlier. You can do this even if you have already started visualizing the worst possible outcome of your situation. You just need to remind yourself that it's far more likely that things will turn out for the best.

There are lots of different ways to do this and they don't all work for everyone. One method that I find really helpful is called the 'Stop,

Observe and Descartes' technique. You start by stop thinking about whatever concerns you, so that your mind is free to focus on something else. Observe means that you refrain from thinking negative thoughts and stop worrying about whatever it was that concerned you. And finally, by remembering your favorite philosopher you can remind yourself that these negative feelings will pass and rationality will return once again. For me, I think of the famous French philosopher René Descartes and remember his famous maxim 'I think, therefore I am'.

Visualize A Positive Outcome

This technique requires some sacrifice on your part but it can definitely help to boost your confidence in how you deal with intrusive thoughts. You need to imagine a positive outcome from any situation, whether or not anything goes wrong. You can do this by picturing the situation going perfectly well, and then by thinking about what you could do to make sure that things go well. This might sound completely ridiculous, but it's a great way to stop yourself from worrying about all of those negative possibilities. It takes some practice but it's worth it in the end!

Use Your Imagination

I know from my own experience that your imagination can be a pretty scary place to be. But this is where you need to start if you want to overcome those intrusive thoughts. You need to learn how to recognize when your mind is wandering into these negative thought patterns and, as soon as you notice it, make a conscious effort to steer your mind away from them.

This is important because these intrusive thoughts are all too easy to get carried away by - and it can be hard to pull yourself out of these negative thoughts. You will start with a single thought that worries you and then somehow convince yourself that things are going wrong. So when you notice these negative thoughts coming on, you need to do your best to stop yourself. This can be really tricky to do but it will get easier as time passes.

Use All Your Senses

This is something that I wish I had achieved years ago, but I'm still working on it now! It's sometimes hard to understand what exactly you feel when you have intrusive thoughts and this can make it hard to combat them from the inside. This is where learning how to use all of your senses when dealing with these negative thoughts can help immensely, because it takes some of the focus off of your thoughts and puts more emphasis on what's going on around you.

You can use the visual sense by visualizing a scenario where you are thinking these thoughts and then make sure that you imagine what it looks like. This is also helpful if you're trying to concentrate for an exam or some other important task - by imagining your focus will get distracted by any stray thoughts that come into your head.

You can use the auditory sense as well, so that you know when your mind has been wandering away from the task at hand; listen to a repetitive sound, such as a song, and imagine yourself being angry every time you hear it. This is a good way to remind you of the physical sensations that you are going through and how they are affecting your mind.

You can also use smell, taste, touch and even taste by using aromatic or edible substances to help distract yourself from intrusive thought patterns. These are all good ways that you will be able to keep your mind focused on what's outside of it without having to think about these intrusive thoughts.

Use a Mental Trigger

This is one technique that I find really helpful for interrupting or shifting my focus away from intrusive thoughts once they have started. A mental trigger is something that you can use as a reminder for when you notice yourself having those thoughts - and it can be a small physical action or sound that reminds you of what these thoughts are about. You can use the things that your mind comes up with to remind you of the real problem.

For example, one of my intrusive thought patterns is that my house might catch on fire. This is a horrible thought to have, so I need something that will remind me about this idea.

So, I've got an alarm clock in my bedroom which goes off at the same time every night. Whenever I hear it, I remember how awful this intrusive thought is and remind myself to think about something else.

Use Reminders

This can be another way of using a mental trigger to remind you of these negative thoughts, since it's essentially the same thing. This technique involves attaching items or objects to yourself that will remind you of these intrusive thoughts so that you can immediately stop thinking about them when you notice them. You can also use bodily sensations (like pins and needles) as reminders when they happen; if your leg falls asleep (or some other part), that means that your mind is wandering into a negative thought pattern. And if you can stop yourself thinking about whatever it is you're worrying about then your body should start feeling normal again. This might sound confusing but it works for me!

Take a Timeout

Or you can use some kind of barrier to separate your mind from what's going on around it. Whether you need to be away from the person that triggers your thoughts, or just away from whatever is going on in the present situation, this is a really simple technique that will help. You don't have to necessarily do anything during this time, other than allow yourself to think about something else for a little while.

If you need to be away from the person that is making you worry about these intrusive thoughts, you need to try and distract yourself from them - this is one technique I cannot recommend enough! This can be really difficult to do for some people but it's one of the most helpful techniques in my opinion.

Meditate

I'm a big fan of meditation. I don't think that it's a bad thing at all - there's no way that anyone should feel pressured into meditating or doing any other kind of relaxation technique if they're not ready for it. But I do think that meditation can be a really helpful technique for dealing with intrusive thoughts - especially if you are getting yourself hyped up by something else and have a hard time concentrating on them.

Whenever you are having intrusive thoughts, simply start with longer periods of meditation to help you relax a bit and settle the mind down. This will stop your intrusive thoughts from going off into the background and completely overtaking your mind as you concentrate on them. There are many different kinds of meditation but there are two techniques that I really like; one is called chi kung (or "energy work") and the other is what's known as "open-monitoring".

Practice Gratitude

I really like to do this - especially if I've had a rough day with intrusive thoughts. All you need to do is think of everything that you have done or are going to do that day - this will help keep your mind sharp but it will also remind you of all of the things in your life that you can be grateful for. If you're not feeling thankful for something, then try and ask yourself what exactly it is that you're thinking about and why it's making you scared or anxious. Is there anything in your life that you really wish that you didn't have to worry about? If so, try and spend a few minutes thinking about why you're thinking this way; you'll be surprised by what it is.

By focusing on these things it will help your mind to calm; it will give you some perspective. You might even find that you don't even need to meditate or go running as much as I do - just taking a minute or two every day to think about all of the good things in your life can do wonders for calming the mind.

If I have a bad day then I use these techniques often - they allow me to focus on something else and not let my worries get away from me. I'll take a few minutes to think about something nice that happened, or something that I have to be grateful for, or just think about the things that I need to do the next day.

Focus on one thing at a time and it will help your mind to calm down considerably - this is something you can do while you're at work or in some other environment. Even if it's just for a few minutes, thinking of all of the different things that you should be grateful for can help your mind more than you'd ever expect.

In Summary

There's no single best way to deal with them - it depends on who you are and what kind of thoughts you have. But if one thing stands out to you, don't be afraid to try it out for yourself! If nothing else, the techniques that I listed above should give you some good ideas on how to handle these issues when they pop up and hopefully make your life just a bit easier.

Dealing With Self-Harm Thoughts and Feelings

Intrusive thoughts and even OCD. Can be scary, but for some people the idea of harming themselves and others is something that they worry about too. This can be a really hard thing to deal with - especially if you're not used to having these types of thoughts. But after hearing about all of the things that other people have gone through in this book, I've decided to try my best to share my experiences with you as well! There's one main difference with self-harm though: there aren't too many people who will talk about it openly.

Everyone has their own experiences with intrusive thoughts and self-harm; I'm not trying to take over or speak for someone else. On top of that, there are people who have had these thoughts but have never acted on them - not everyone is actually suicidal. But for the people who do act on their thoughts, it can be scary to decide how to deal with them.

All About Self-Harm - Why It Happens and What to Do About It

One of the scariest things about intrusive thoughts and self-harm is that they can seem alien. People might wonder "why would anyone want to hurt themselves?" or "who would want to commit suicide?" The truth is - it really isn't that simple. Even if someone has never had a thought about self-harm in their life, they might still want to do it! Not everyone who tries to harm themselves actually does - but the thoughts don't always come from you.

Think about this: you're sitting by yourself thinking about self-harm - what are the chances of you actually doing it? Probably not very high. But what if you were alone with someone else and they said something like:

"oh my god, I think that Brad is going to do some serious self-harm right now. He's really depressed". If you were still sitting by yourself then you might not even notice what the other person was talking about - but now that you have a third person in the room, it suddenly makes you think twice!

If this happened to me then I would instantly start thinking about how I would deal with that situation. The other person would try and talk me down from it, and I would be wondering if they were just lying to me to make me feel better. But it turns out that this is literally exactly how thoughts about self-harm work - they're not always your own thoughts; if somebody else says something like that to you then it can change your mind and give you what are sometimes called "mental sensations".

Nerve-wracking, intrusive thoughts may pop into your mind at any moment. You literally can't take a shower without being bombarded by unwanted, anxious thoughts. If you are struggling to get out of bed in the morning because you're having negative or obsessive thought loops, it's time to end it for good!

Studies have shown that hypnosis can be used in a therapeutic setting to not only reduce anxiety but also change the way we react to stressful situations. Researchers found that people who were trained in self-hypnosis techniques were better able to cope with stressful situations and had less tumultuous reactions than those who did not use the techniques.

Lead author of the study, Stephen K. Rice, Ph.D., explains, "It appears that people who have the ability to self-induce hypnosis can use it to influence their responses to a variety of situations..." The research suggests that training yourself in self-hypnosis may help you cope with anxiety-provoking situations.

In addition, hypnosis has been used successfully by adults and children as a way to learn coping strategies for managing unwanted thoughts and feelings caused by chronic pain or other debilitating illnesses. In the past decade, hypnotherapy has also been shown effective in reducing anxiety and stress in people coping with serious illness or undergoing major surgery.

Given that hypnosis can effectively reduce the anxiety levels of those suffering from stress, how does it work? The mind has a split-second "fight or flight" response which is set off when we are in dangerous or threatening situations. However, many stressors do not present us with an immediate or direct physical threat. Consequently, the brain has developed an elaborate defense system to help reduce the anxiety of these situations.

This defense system involves activating our unconscious perception and attribution system, a part of the mind which is linked to our past experiences and memories. Our unconscious perceptions are linked to our past experiences through a subconscious link that maintains automatic thoughts and associations to events. The unconscious system is controlled by the autonomic nervous system, which controls involuntary actions.

When we are in a stressful situation, our body generates adrenaline. This causes the heart to beat faster and the blood vessels to constrict, narrowing peripheral vision. While it appears that the only purpose of activating this response is to increase physical and mental alertness by getting us into a fight or flight mode, this reaction actually has a doubleedged response.

Consequently, our unconscious does not stop there! It also generates automatic thoughts and associations to these stressful situations which seem to occur in an instant as soon as the threat detector activates. These automatic thoughts can cause a negative and distorted perception of the situation, which in turn causes additional anxiety.

With the hindsight of knowing what happens to our minds during a stressful situation, it becomes clear why hypnosis and self-hypnosis can be effective in reducing anxiety. By consciously guiding your unconscious system into a deeper state of relaxation as you are being hypnotized, you can then take control over your thoughts.

The result is that where once there was an automatic response in your mind and body to certain things, it now becomes easier for you to make different associations or have new perspectives on these situations. This will help you reduce the emotional impact of stress or illness by reducing or even eliminating its harmful impact on you psychologically.

How Hypnosis Reduces Anxiety

In hypnosis for anxiety, the conscious mind is brought into a very relaxed state while the subconscious mind is guided to take over and take control. This conscious-subconscious connection will allow you to make more intelligent decisions and act accordingly in order to reduce your stress and anxiety.

In addition, hypnosis using self-hypnosis allows you to give yourself effective coping mechanisms and techniques that can be used in everyday life. This will help you feel more confident as well as having greater control over your thoughts by creating a positive mental attitude towards whatever it is that causes you stress or anxiety.

Long-term results: The real benefit of hypnosis is the longer-term effect you can achieve. Through hypnotherapy, you can learn to eliminate a lot of stress and anxiety before it even reaches the surface. Instead, it will be neutralized on a more unconscious level, which will make it much easier for you to do what is necessary to cope with this stress or anxiety.

How effective is hypnotherapy for anxiety?

It is difficult to tell exactly how effective hypnotherapy will be for your particular stress and anxiety. However, it has been proven to be consistently beneficial in a wide variety of situations. In fact, hypnotherapy is commonly used to treat stress and anxiety due to the high degree of effectiveness that it tends to have.

Hypnosis is also highly recommended as there are few side effects compared with other treatments for stress and anxiety, like antidepressants. Although some people report feeling energized after a session or even feeling tired as they do not want to leave the trance state, many people claim that they feel much calmer after a session than before they came into the office.

In addition, many people report feeling more confident and empowered to handle stressful situations with ease afterward, which is a great benefit. Hypnotherapy is not going to be for everyone, but if you are interested in trying it out, there are classes that can be taken over the course of a few weeks or even months to help ensure that you understand the process and how it works on your mind.

Chapter 3 Learn Mindfulness Skills to Cope With Depression-Related Challenges—One Deep, Cleansing Breath at A Time

Learn Mindfulness Skills to Cope With Depression

The 5-Minute Guide to Use Mindfulness and Happiness to Overcome Depression & Anxiety

We all know one person who has problems with anxiety and this person is you. More than half the American population suffers from anxiety at some point in their life. Many people are still unaware of ways to cope with it, which leads to damaged relationships, health problems, and eventually medication. Mindfulness is a set of skills that increase awareness of thoughts, feelings, and sensations to help achieve peace of mind. When our mind is calm, we can feel more relaxed and confident.

Mindfulness is usually developed through meditation. There are many different styles of meditation but the most important thing you need to know about them all is that they all emphasize being present at the moment without judgment or negativity. All of these techniques are meant for long-term use so you can use them for years to come whether your anxiety happens at night or during the day. The technique that I personally prefer is the Awareness Style because it emphasizes awareness and being mindful of what the moment actually feels like. What does it feel like right now to your heart rate? How does this feeling affect your body, mind, and spirit?

In order to learn mindfulness skills, you need to develop attention. Attention is a skill that everyone needs to improve as we grow up because the more we focus on something, the better we can focus.

Here are the 7 most important steps that are crucial for improving concentration: 1) Sleep Well – We all know how difficult it is to get a good night's sleep when anxiety or depression strikes. The most important thing you can do for yourself is to make a plan to sleep well regularly. Make sure that you walk or exercise before bed. Stress and anxiety can easily cause heart rate and blood pressure to rise during the day. Take time to relax your muscles by stretching, doing yoga, or meditating before bedtime. If you wake up during the night and can't fall back to sleep, try reading a book instead of watching TV which could keep your mind activated. 2) Exercise – In addition to light resistance training, yoga is very good at lowering stress levels in the body. Stretching can also help reduce tension in the body. It is important to remember that you should not exercise more than once or twice a day. Overworking your muscles during the day can lead to an overworked heart and a weak immune system. 3) Drink Water – Consuming too much water is not good for your body because it can cause significant amounts of dehydration. When you begin to feel that you are becoming dehydrated, stop drinking water until you feel better; otherwise, it could cause more harm than good by over-drying your body. 4) Meditation – There are many different ways to meditate but I personally chose this style because it is easy to remember and practice daily. Here is a quick 5-minute guide to mindfulness that you can follow for relief from anxiety:

1) Sit in a comfortable position with your back straight. Don't slouch! 2) Close your eyes and take a few deep breaths. Feel the air filling the bottom of your lungs up to your chest. 3) For the next 5 minutes, focus on your breathing and nothing else. If thoughts come into your head just let them go and bring yourself back to focus on the breath.

If you follow this style of breathing consistently, you will notice changes in mood and relief from anxiety in about 2 weeks.

Mindfulness skills are not only about practicing breathing techniques. In order to keep stress levels down, you need to learn other ways to cope with anxiety in your everyday life. For example, after you shower, try slowing down and taking a few deep breaths before you dry your hair. If someone calls you asking for money early in the morning, don't remind yourself of your bills until right before you leave your bedroom. Take a couple of deep breaths while you are eating breakfast and remember that whenever possible, eat slowly and stop eating when your stomach is full. Do not overindulge in sugar as this can make anxiety worse. Throughout the day, notice the different places that cause anxiety for you. Is it while you are driving? At work? In the grocery store? Once you notice these triggers, take a couple of deep breaths to calm your body and mind before going into each situation.

You can follow this 5-minute guide every day until your anxiety is under control. It will take practice and patience but if you stay consistent, you can feel relieved of anxiety in as soon as 2 weeks! Remember that there are many ways to cope with depression and anxiety. Please do not give up because sometimes it takes a while for things to get better.

If you have practiced these daily mindfulness skills that I shared earlier but still feel like your mood is not getting any better, then perhaps you need more support. You can ask for help from a mental health professional or talk to a trusted friend about your situation. If you don't feel comfortable talking to someone, there are many resources available such as the Anxiety and Depression Association of America (ADAA) and the Canadian Mental Health Association (CMHA). Last but not least, remember that you do not have to suffer in silence! You have the power to change your life for the better through hard work and dedication.

Learn Mindfulness Skills to Cope With Related Challenges

My life has been a struggle with anxiety and I'm not alone. Anxiety affects tens of millions of people around the world and many people are dealing with symptoms similar to my own, including poor sleep, loss of appetite, irritability, and more.

Learn mindfulness skills from renowned international experts to cope with anxiety in your life. From calming down during a fight or teaching your kids how to cope when you're feeling overwhelmed at school, check out our list below for some tried-and-true solutions that work as well as they sound.

1. Breathing exercises to calm yourself

When you feel the urge to get panicky keep this simple but effective breathing exercise in mind:

Take a few deep breaths. Inhale through your nose for four counts and exhale for two counts. Repeat for at least 10 breaths. Now switch your focus onto your hands, close your eyes and take four slow, long breaths with the same method above, doing this for at least two minutes. Relax completely and repeat the whole sequence one more time.

2. Meditation

When you're struggling with anxiety, take a moment to meditate. Just five minutes every day can make a tremendous difference.

There are many meditation techniques but I've personally found the following to be the most effective for me:

Sit quietly and clear your mind of all thoughts. When an anxious thought comes in or your mind keeps wandering, just acknowledge it and return to focus on your breath. Power through any negative self-talk that may come up; nothing you tell yourself is true, after all. Inhale deeply for four counts and exhale for six counts until you feel calm and centered again. If any negative thoughts still occur in your mind, just repeat this step until you feel in control again.

3. Appreciate the little things

Have you ever picked up a yellow leaf from the sidewalk and held it in your hand, either to snap a photo or just look at it? Think back on that moment. Was there any panic that went along with it? Probably not, but did you still appreciate the color of the leaf or take time to look at it and think about how fragile nature is?

What about the moment you looked up at the sky and its beautiful colors or smelled a flower on a rare spring day? These are all examples of things for which I cannot help but be grateful—and for which I choose to remind myself in times of stress.

4. Learn about your emotions

Learn about the emotions that are causing you concern and understand why you are feeling the way you do. It's not a matter of "should" doing this, it's an issue of "need to". By taking the time to learn about yourself, you'll be better prepared to understand what emotions are prompting anxiety or other negative feelings.

5. Exercise at least 30 minutes every day

Exercise is good for us in every way, especially if we exercise regularly—and it works well for anxiety as well. Physically, exercise can boost our moods and help us get rid of stress and anxiety. If you're new to exercising, it's best to start with a short period and work your way up to 30 minutes a day.

6. Practice yoga

Yoga is something that I've been doing for years, and it's produced incredible results for my physical, mental, and emotional health. The beauty of yoga is that it asks us to slow down and feel the present moment. This gives us time to become aware of the thoughts we think—and that we can choose not to think any negative thoughts if we don't want to! Yoga teaches us how to be mindful so that we can live in peace with ourselves and those around us.

7. Accept your anxious feelings

When I feel anxious, I want to run away and hide. It's important for me to know that it's okay to feel this way and that there's nothing wrong with me. Anxiety isn't something you

should be ashamed of or afraid of, especially if you have a mental illness, which is treatable.
8. Don't fight against your feelings

When you go through difficult times it can be tempting to push against them or fight them off at all costs—and sometimes we succeed! But when we do fight our feelings instead of accepting our negative emotions, they only become stronger over time. Our bodies need peace to heal, so giving yourself a break from anxious thoughts and feelings might just give you the space you need to find sanity again. 9. Don't compare yourself to others

This is a major mistake we all make when feeling anxious. I know for myself, sometimes even good friends will compare themselves to others or tell me how unhappy they are and how "things are so much worse than you guys" because of anxiety. What they don't realize is that everyone has their own set of challenges coming up in life—and they can all be dealt with in different ways! Anxiety isn't a punishment for being an ordinary person, it's just one of the struggles we all have in life at times. Everyone is different and everyone has their own things to worry about.

Decide to be kind and supportive toward friends and family who suffer from anxiety. They need it most of all.

10. Educate others about your disorder

Educate the people in your life on what it's like to live with anxiety—and how you've worked hard to live a full life despite being affected by it. Educating people who are close to us is a great way to help those around us understand our situations, and in the end, make them more compassionate toward what we're going through.

Learn Mindfulness Skills to Cope With One Deepest Fears

Anxiety is a common mental disorder that affects many people. It is characterized by the feeling of fear, worry or unease, and physical manifestations such as racing heart rate, trembling and nausea. In extreme cases it can lead to panic attacks.

There are many techniques to help treat anxiety disorders but one popular option remains the practice of mindfulness. Mindfulness is an ancient Buddhist meditation technique that teaches us to be in the present moment without judgment and free from worries about the future or regrets about the past. This way of living has proven beneficial for those suffering from various forms of anxiety, like generalized anxiety disorder (GAD), post-traumatic stress disorder (PTSD) and obsessive-compulsive disorder (OCD).

In the last decade, scientists have found that practicing mindfulness meditation regularly can reduce anxiety and stress in people. This is because the practice of mindfulness meditation requires sustained awareness and introspective thinking about your past, present, and future thoughts. It also helps you gain a clearer perspective on your feelings and moods.

Mindfulness as self-help

For most people like you and I who suffer from anxiety disorders, the most important aspect of mindfulness is its use as a tool to treat anxiety symptoms.

The foundation of mindfulness practice is the establishment of the different elements that contribute to it. These can be said as its pillars. The following are the main pillars of mindfulness:

1. Mindfulness meditation – The first step in practicing meditation is simply to close your eyes and focus on your breath for a few minutes every day, not to clear your mind but to develop a habit and familiarity with concentration techniques. This will help you develop your concentration skills for mindfulness. There are many kinds of meditation; you can use any method (e.g. breathing, mantra, visualization) as long as it works for you.

2. Mindfulness in your daily life – After establishing a foundation of mindfulness techniques, you can now begin to integrate the tools into your everyday life. Try and be mindful when you're doing daily chores, such as washing the dishes or doing laundry – notice what is happening around you without judgment or attachments. You can also take any activity where you can almost guarantee to feel anxiety (e.g. an interview) and do it mindfully to experience less anxiety when it comes time for the real thing.

3. Mindfulness for treating anxiety disorders – Those with anxiety disorders often have difficulty feeling the present moment and are

constantly worrying about their state of mind in the future or feeling regretful about past mistakes. To counter this, you can also practice mindfulness techniques as a way to help you become more aware of your thoughts. Mindfulness meditation helps relieve anxiety by clearing your mind of negative thoughts, making room for positive ones and making you feel more compassionate about others.

Those suffering from anxiety disorders should consult their local physician or therapist before beginning a mindfulness meditation schedule. This is because some individuals with anxiety are in a constant state of stress, making it easy to tire out easily during a meditation session and be vulnerable to feelings of depression or resentment. You must also be ready to commit yourself to practice meditation regularly for months or even years to experience full benefits.

Learn Mindfulness Skills to Cope With One Deep

There are many techniques to help treat anxiety disorders but one popular option remains the practice of mindfulness. Mindfulness is an ancient Buddhist meditation technique that teaches us to be in the present moment without judgment and free from worries about the future or regrets about the past. This way of living has proven beneficial for those suffering from various forms of anxiety, like generalized anxiety disorder (GAD), post-traumatic stress disorder (PTSD) and obsessive-compulsive disorder (OCD).

Learn Mindfulness Skills to Cope With Cleansing Breath at a Time of Anxiety

When your anxiety attacks, the calming and centering breathing techniques that you learned in an Emotional Freedom Technique tapping session can be the most helpful tool to help your anxiety subside. The breath is a natural and easy way to calm yourself and it can be incredibly effective for many people with anxiety. Here are some routines you can use to practice these calming breathing techniques.

#2 - Intentionally Count Your Breath for 4 Seconds

As soon as you notice your body start to tense, it is important that you take deep breaths into your diaphragm instead of shallow breaths through your mouth which will only increase the tension in your body. It is also important to practice the skill of counting. These are things that can be done while you are driving or sitting in a waiting room which will distract your mind from anxious thoughts.

Intentionally take 4 seconds to inhale and 4 seconds to exhale. If you find yourself thinking of something other than how the breath feels, start again at one as if you have lost count. Also, this is part of what is called a 'mindfulness' breathing technique because you are being intentionally aware of your breath at that present moment.

#3 - Intentionally Count Your Breath for 8 Seconds

As before, intentionally take 8 seconds to inhale and 8 seconds to exhale. When you are trying to be mindful, the idea is that you are only focusing on the breath - nothing else. If you're feeling your anxiety rising, stop what you're doing and practice this breathing technique. Again, if your mind wanders from the breath, start over at one.

#4 - Practice Mindful Breathing While You Walk

You can practice mindful breathing while walking as long as your mind isn't wandering all over the place. Before you get started, make sure to walk in a mindful manner by and focusing on your body.

#5 - Practice Breathing While Writing

Next, you can practice this while writing as long as your mind isn't wandering. Before you get down to writing, take a few deep breaths.

Make sure that you concentrate on your breathing while doing so and that it is only the breath that is being attended to. Sometimes people who have terrible handwriting can still benefit from this breathing technique and it's easier to focus on the process of writing while concentrating on the breath.

#6 - Practice Mindful Breathing While Eating

You can also practice mindful breathing while eating as long as your mind isn't wandering all over the place. Before you get started, you can do this in conjunction with using the Emotional

Freedom Technique tapping technique. Have you ever noticed that when you are anxious and find yourself with a full plate of food (because of your anxieties of course), that despite having eaten healthy all week, you suddenly feel very anxious? This is because of your body's inability to digest food properly when anxious which causes nausea.

You can practice mindful breathing while eating as long as your mind isn't wandering all over the place. Before you get started, you can do this in conjunction with using the Emotional Freedom Technique tapping technique. Have you ever noticed that when you are anxious and find yourself with a full plate of food (because of your anxieties of course), that despite having eaten healthy all week, you suddenly feel very anxious? This is because of your body's inability to digest food properly when anxious which causes nausea.

This is the perfect time to practice this breathing technique! You can actually practice this while eating and still be mindful because your mind won't be focused on anything other than the meal in front of you at that moment in time. You can also practice this while eating and drinking water, another anxiety trigger that causes me to feel nauseous.

#7 - Practice Mindful Breathing While Walking Around Your House

The next routine is one that allows you to practice mindful breathing without any distraction while walking around the house in a mindful manner. You can practice this while doing chores, like cleaning the garage or walking your dog.

#8 - Practice Mindful Breathing While Sitting In the Waiting Room or At a Doctors Office

Often when I have an appointment to go to with my doctor, I find myself becoming very anxious. This is because I don't really want to go. I suspect it's the same for many people out there who find themselves in a similar situation. What you can do in this situation is practice breathing mindfully while sitting in the waiting room or at your doctor's office and focusing on how your body feels without that anxiety attacking you.

#9 - Use High Energy Tapping When Your Anxiety Is High

When you are feeling anxious and low energy, like you don't care about anything, it is important to think back to when your anxiety was low and then tap accordingly. This will help you tap into the high-energy state and get out of a low-energy place.

#10 - If Anxious, Don't Do the Things You Usually Do To Soothe Your Anxiety

When you feel anxiety rising, it is important to think about what you usually do to calm yourself down. Do you get in your car and listen to music or head home and watch TV? The problem with these approaches is that they are all passive activities where your mind can wander. By removing yourself from these triggers, you take away the ability for your mind to wander and aggravate itself. You also take away the opportunity for your anxieties from rising.

#11 - Accept What's Happening

Often when we look at how we feel, we assume that the feelings are a reality and therefore something that we need to change or get rid of. This is not true. We need to realize that what is going on in our mind is not necessarily true and that any thoughts you have about yourself are only useful for your thoughts, not reality. It's important to realize that the way you feel at this moment in time is NOT permanent - it will pass and the better you accept it right now, the easier it will be for you in the future.

Chapter 4 Discover Words of Encouragement as You Build the Confidence, Self-Acceptance, and Clarity You Need In Order To Break Free Of Depression-Related Thought Patterns and Create Lasting Change

Overcoming anxiety and depression is the toughest battle anyone will ever face. It exhausts you and can be crippling to your mental and physical well-being. You need the inspiration, knowledge, and tools in order to win this fight — but they're not always readily available.

What is an anxiety or depression recovery tip from the "self-help" community that actually works?

The answer is quite simple: words of encouragement.

Words of encouragement are undeniably powerful but have a very subtle and hard to define effect. You need to know how to use them effectively if you want to achieve significant results in your own battle against depression and anxiety. I'll explain its benefits, how it works, and why you need it in your life.

First, Let's Define Our Terms

What is an anxiety attack?

An anxiety attack is a sudden, intense moment of panic and fear. It is caused by your body's natural fight or flight response. The symptoms aren't immediate but they are present in the moment you first experience it. You'll often feel overwhelmed and have trouble breathing, be noticeably cold, or even break out into a sweat. Most people describe their attacks as a sudden surge of negative emotions and overwhelming thoughts that can easily consume you in an instant.

What is depression? There are two types of depression: clinical and non-clinical depression. Clinical depression is a serious mental disorder that can surface after a person has had their fair share of bad life events. The symptoms of clinical depression are extreme sadness, happiness, exhaustion, and an inability to function almost normally. All clinical depression symptoms can strike at any given time in your life. You may experience this momentary damage to your well-being all on its own or after the effects of another major event in your life.

What is anxiety? Anxiety appears very often as an emotion you experience in conjunction with depression. It's a different beast altogether though because it can be experienced daily without any triggers whatsoever and may not be connected at all to another issue in your life. It's just a feeling-in-general that your body creates naturally. That said, anxiety can be triggered by a situation or experience in the immediate moment.

Benefits of Using Words of Encouragement in Depression and Anxiety Recovery

Words of encouragement are powerful because they provide you with an immediate mental lifting effect that can be sustained throughout the day. They give you an upbeat attitude that you need in order to combat negative thoughts and remain in control over your mental suffering. The best part is it only takes seconds for this eloquent boost to happen. Words of encouragement are so easy to use that it's almost laughable. All you have to do is think of a positive thing you want to say, write it down or speak it aloud, and hold that thought in your head throughout the day.

These words lift your spirits and create a mood of positivity that will last for hours afterward. It's like an instant shot of energy from inside your head that will keep you motivated, energized, and lifting those spirits. This mental boost will give you a great attitude towards yourself and your life — boosting motivation, confidence, self-esteem, and determination — which is exactly what we need in order to get through depression and anxiety recovery.

How to Use Words Of Encouragement Effectively

Whenever you find yourself in a negative, anxious, or depressed state of mind, use these words to immediately lift your spirits. You don't have to make any sense of them or even know why you're saying them. You just need to create a positive chant in your head that turns your thoughts around and puts you on the right track towards recovery. The most important thing is you need to do whatever it takes to stay positive because there's no other alternative but having depression or anxiety go away correctly. If you allow it, this disease will take over and destroy your life forever – if not sooner. It's really that simple when applying these words properly.

The Benefits of Words of Encouragement in Your Recovery

Words of encouragement are far and away from the best tool for depression and anxiety recovery. You also know that there are people who still don't believe in or understand how beneficial words of encouragement can be when applied correctly.

The first benefit of using words of encouragement in your depression and anxiety recovery is that they will help you get through the day. You're in a battle to save your life, so you need to use all the weapons at your disposal. Words of encouragement are a great weapon against depression and anxiety because they can give you an immediate lift in spirit that will last long after any other mental treatment or technique has worn out its effectiveness.

You can use words of encouragement to power through bad days, relieve stress that's bothering you at the moment, and make it through what feels like a never-ending rough patch in your life. The best part is it only takes seconds to see results – much faster than any other technique you may be using right now.

These words can also help you get your mind off negative thoughts and create a much more relaxed state of being. This is especially helpful if you've had a hard day at work or dealing with daily hassles like traffic jams, rude people, an annoying landlord or neighbor, etc.

The second benefit of using these words in your depression and anxiety recovery is that they will give you hope for the future. Words of encouragement will give you more motivation and confidence to face the future head-on, get out there and live again, and experience life the way it was meant to be lived. You may not be able to change your circumstances at this moment, but you still have a choice in how you choose to deal with them. Anxiety and depression have no control over your future wellbeing – only you do. Now is the time to make that choice as clear as possible.

The third benefit of using words of encouragement in your depression and anxiety recovery is that they will help you gain a deeper understanding of who you are. These words remind us of our inner strength and power we possess when we're well again. They reflect how strong of a person we are when we're fighting for something so important — our own life. These words give us hope for the future and also help us realize that we can make it through anything that comes our way. It's not easy, but it's definitely possible when using these words correctly.

The fourth benefit of using these words in your depression and anxiety recovery is that they will take you out of your comfort zone. This is absolutely necessary if you're going to get well from depression or anxiety and learn to live a normal life again. If you stay in your comfort zone, you're going to have a hard time getting better because this can only happen if you put yourself out there and try new things. This is where words of encouragement shine the brightest because they are a step outside the box.

Being uncomfortable is what makes us stronger as people than those who never have to make a choice in their life – because they don't even have to live in their own realities. The best thing about it is that it's easy to use these words to help you grow in your own personal boundaries for the better. Words of encouragement are an excellent tool for boosting this process so that it becomes a habit for you over time – until your boundaries expand so wide that they become our reality.

The fifth benefit of using these words in your depression and anxiety recovery is that they will help you get over the fear of getting better. This may not be the case for everyone, but it is definitely true for many people who are suffering from this disease. Depression and anxiety can make us fearful of making a change — even if it means getting better. You don't want to put yourself out there because you're afraid of what may happen next when you get out of your comfort zone.

This fear can also prevent you from taking action which means the condition never gets better because you're always waiting for the "right time" to do something. There's no right time or wrong time, there's only whatever time you choose to make it happen. This is why using words of encouragement can help you deal with the fear of change because they'll make you more comfortable with taking action and move forward towards your life goals without hesitating any longer.

The sixth benefit of using these words in your depression and anxiety recovery is that they will help keep you motivated to stay positive during depressive phases. This is important when we're in a battle with mental illness and need to use all our energy to recover successfully. You're going to feel great relief when you learn how these words can work for you mentally – even when it's not feeling so great emotionally.

Remember that you're never alone in this battle. In fact, you could be surrounded by someone who's struggling with depression and anxiety and doesn't know what to do about it. Leave them a note or card which says: "You're loved. Keep fighting. I'll help you anytime. Never give up." It just takes a little time and money to get the right tools for the job done right, but it's definitely worth the investment because your future self would thank you for it if they could speak to you face-to-face today.

The seventh benefit of using these words in your depression and anxiety recovery is that they will help you live again. These are words of encouragement that can change someone's life forever. They are a gift to yourself that will last a lifetime — whether it's today, tomorrow, or next week. These are words for the quiet moments when we need them most – when we sit down to reflect on our life and how it unfolded so far, or when we're trying to clear an idea from our minds by typing it down – just like how you're doing right now.

These words can provide comfort and peace in times of struggle through their sound and meaning. They will ease the pains you're feeling right now and will give you the strength to continue moving forward into a future of better days. After all, these words are there for you when they're needed most – when you feel like giving up, when you feel like giving in, or when life feels like too much. Words of encouragement are always there to help us get through those tough times and become stronger people in the process.

The eighth benefit of using these words in your depression and anxiety recovery is that they'll help you overcome any negative effects of your past mistakes. When we're depressed or anxious, we tend to hold onto our past mistakes and regret them like they were really hurting us right now. These words of encouragement will help you do this through their sound and meaning.

They are used to remind you that your past is only a part of the story and that your future can be bright if you don't let these mistakes take over your life. Make sure to use these words as often as possible because they're going to help you set yourself free from a damaged past – which could hold you back in your present state of depression and anxiety.

The ninth benefit of using these words in your depression and anxiety recovery is that they will make you a better person. If you're suffering from depression and anxiety, you want to be a better person. You want to be stronger and healthier which is why you're reading this right now. These words are going to help you take the next step in your life because they'll make you a more compassionate person who doesn't judge others for their past mistakes – because every one of us has them.

These words will help guide your feet along the right path because it's what we should all be doing anyway – learning from our mistakes and never repeating them. When we truly understand this through these words, we'll become much stronger people than those who don't ever use them.

The tenth benefit of using these words in your depression and anxiety recovery is that they will help you feel better about yourself. You're suffering from depression and/or anxiety right now which means you may be feeling ashamed for how you've been acting or behaving – like you should have done something more to prevent the situation from happening. You may even feel like it's all your fault because of the choices you've made – which isn't true at all.

These words will help you realize that all of these negative feelings are completely hogwash. You're not alone and you never were – everyone has made mistakes in their life. You can't change the past but you can definitely learn from it and change your future for the better by using these words to keep your spirit up and to keep going when your spirit is down.

The eleventh benefit of using these words in your depression and anxiety recovery is that they'll motivate you to do more inner work. In order to overcome depression and anxiety, we need to focus on ourselves by doing some inner work. These words will help you do this because they can give you the inspiration you need to continue moving forward into recovery – through them.

These words are going to make you a stronger person and they'll help make your life better. You're going to get better because of these words. You're going to start feeling good about yourself and not feel like your depression and anxiety is tearing you down as much as it used to because now, the only things that are tearing you down are your thoughts – not what's going on in the outside world or how others are treating you.

The twelfth benefit of using these words in your depression and anxiety recovery is that they will help you take control of your life again. We all need to take control of our lives again – it's no secret. These words will help you do this by getting your mind on the right track again so that you can see that you have a say in how things are going to go in your life.

You're not at the mercy of others and you never were. You have control over what happens to you because you have a say in what happens. These words will help remind you of that power inside your mind, body, and soul so that it can be used to motivate yourself into overcoming depression and anxiety more and more every day until these feelings fade away completely – allowing you to take control of your life for good.

There are times when the anxiety...the fear...the feeling of being overwhelmed is so intense you can't deal with it. It's paralyzing and overwhelming and you just need a moment to breathe before taking the next step. But sometimes it's not that simple, something triggers an onslaught of panic in our minds and we're completely afraid of what will happen if we try to slow it down or catch our breath. The more you experience these types of situations, the more likely they'll be to occur again in your life; your mind always wants to escape from something that scares us into thinking we ll never be able to overcome it. But you can learn to change your thoughts and even if it seems impossible at that moment, you really can overcome them.

You Can Build Self-Acceptance and Self-Confidence

In the midst of anxiety, depression, and panic attacks, self-acceptance is difficult to see for many people. All they see is the overwhelming feeling they have at any given time that makes it impossible for them to feel confident or happy about themselves. The only way out of that feeling is by taking action with a plan. By choosing specific strategies to use, you can create a path to success.

A Few Ways to Start Building Self-Confidence and Self-Acceptance:

Write down a list of reasons why you are important to the people you care about. It could be your family, friends, co-workers or even your pets. Try and list at least 10 and then pick the 5 that are most powerful for you. When you need inspiration, look back on these reasons why they have chosen to be in your life.

If there's something that makes you feel insecure or unable to accept yourself - be it a bad habit - try and think of some positive things that will help encourage positive change.

Think of it this way; if you've had to deal with a panic attack or anxiety over the past months, what have you done to help yourself? Have you given yourself time to breathe, accepted that things are going to get better, and started thinking in a positive way? If so, you can do it again. No matter how often or how badly you feel like taking off from life and struggling with these issues; asking for support, identifying a reason for why you can build self-confidence and self-acceptance will work in your favor.

...and Get The Help You Need!

If your thoughts are paralyzing or overwhelming and feeling suicidal is the only way you know how to cope...then by all means...get the help you need! Whether it's a therapist, counselor, medication, or a combination of all of the above...you need a way to shift your thoughts and make yourself feel better. Without this you won't be able to take action or you'll only feel worse. There are so many things you can do on your own but sometimes putting some work into building yourself back up can be an effective choice. So yes, take action and get the help you need.

There's a lot of negative talk that goes around when people feel like they're not good enough or smart enough or pretty enough to be a part of life. What if you could change all the things about yourself that make it seem like you can't handle life? What if you could learn to look at yourself in a positive way and understand that the things that make you feel insecure are something everyone deals with at some point and time? You have the power to use your thoughts and feelings as an excuse or as something to build on. In order to do this, you have to choose what will work best for you.

At the end of the day, if you're looking for something that can make you feel better, then there's a reason you came to this site. So whether it's because you want to know how to stop anxiety or it's because your thoughts are overwhelming you...there's something out there that can help.

Remember to take action! No matter what kind of meds or therapy works best for your situation, the best thing you can do is start making progress! So grab a piece of paper and a pen and write down all your thoughts and feelings about this...about yourself...about life...and start building yourself back up again. Eventually, it will stop being so hard, you'll realize the things that make you feel insecure aren't all that bad after all and even if they are...you can build yourself back up again.

The good news is...it's so much easier to do than you might think. And all your fears will fade away eventually and you'll start to feel confident again. You'll find yourself thinking about who you are and why your worth it, finding things you love about yourself and accepting the things that make you feel insecure. Your thoughts will become more positive and everything will start to feel better.

The Right Tools Can Make All the Difference

If you want to feel better and build the confidence, self-acceptance, and clarity you need in order to move on from a life filled with anxiety...then it's time to start making a plan. With the right tools, you can create the progress you want so much.

So get out that piece of paper again and start writing down your thoughts about everything mentioned here. Use the questions below as a guide and make sure to spend some time thinking about what each question means...how it makes you feel...and what will help change your perspective on things. Don't forget that while your feelings are important, and they're hard to shift sometimes...they're also not something you have to deal with on your own. You don t have to feel this way. It's always okay to ask for help and there are people out there who want to help.

What's one thing you can do on your own to help yourself? List it here.

What's one thing you would ask a friend to do for you?

What's one thing you need to do in order to move forward with your life?

How can you use those 5 reasons why the people you care about are in your life as motivation?

In order to feel better and get back into your life, what do think about yourself that needs some improvement? Write it here.

It's such a simple thing, but writing down everything that comes to mind will help so much. It lets your brain focus on something else besides your thoughts and puts all of those worries onto paper so that they're out of your head for now.

Now that you've written it down, make sure it's in the right place. Make sure that this is the first thing you think about every morning when you wake up and that it's the last thing you think about before going to bed at night. Do this for 2 weeks in a row and you'll start to see progress. It's okay if you don't feel better yet...you're going to feel so much better. It will happen, but don't get discouraged if it doesn't happen within a couple of months...it takes time to build back up all of those negative feelings.

Learning to Make Progress

The only way to get better is to put some work into it. So write down what you think your thoughts and feelings are and what you would do differently. You can even write down why your thoughts make you feel that way and what advice someone else would give you if they were there with you. If your anxiety is paralyzing or overwhelming then writing things down will help take care of any problem that may be stopping you from taking action. Write this out...then every time after that, write the same thoughts again in the same place on the page and see how much progress you've made.

Chapter 5 Filled With Warm Affirmations

Filled With Warm Affirmations, this is the first in a series of short but powerful self-help guides that will take you from feeling anxious to mastering your anxiety.

Although anxiety seems like it's forever lurking in the shadows, it can easily manifest when things don't go our way. Anxiety is something that we all have to deal with, and sometimes it can even feel like an unbeatable opponent.

But, while it may present itself as an obstacle to overcome, anxiety is really a call for your attention. It is an opportunity to re-evaluate the things you've been doing and how they are affecting you on a deeper level.

The most effective way to conquer your anxiety involves identifying the roots of your fear. You'll gain new self-awareness and insight that will allow you to make more intelligent decisions as a result of that knowledge. Not only that, but I promise you this: once you open yourself up to this information, anxiety loses its ability to control and paralyze you any longer.

"Your feelings and emotions are linked directly back to your thoughts." -Dr. Wayne Dyer

Your Thoughts Have Power

In order to conquer your anxiety, you must first be able to identify what it is that is causing your anxiety. Keep in mind that this is not always easy. We are often completely unaware of what or why we're anxious in the first place. Oftentimes, our anxiety stems from fears we aren't even consciously aware of! As a result, it's critical to dig deep and look for the root cause of your feelings. When you can identify the source of your fear, you can then better understand why you're feeling such a strong sense of anxiety in the first place.

Once you're able to identify the roots of your anxiety, you'll get closer to solving it. You will become aware of your feelings and emotions, and what triggers them. This awareness is the first step to controlling your anxiety.

Prove Your Thoughts Wrong!

Take a moment to write down all of the thoughts that are going through your mind at this very moment. You may say: "But, most of my thoughts are negative! I don't even want to acknowledge them." Trust me...I know. I understand what it feels like to have negative thoughts running through your mind on a daily basis. You may also be thinking: "How can I prove my thoughts wrong if I have to admit that they're even real in the first place?"

It certainly doesn't feel too good to acknowledge your negative thoughts. Most of the time, it's really not easy! But, guess what: you can prove your thoughts wrong...without having to argue with them or constantly try and disprove them. How? By shifting your focus onto a different subject. When you shift your focus, the thought that was previously causing you anxiety shifts and dissipates.

Your thoughts are like clouds in the sky. Sometimes, they hang around for a while. But when the sun comes out, they disappear and are replaced by bright and sunny skies.

"It's not what you look at that matters, it's what you see." -Henry David Thoreau

It Is What You See...Not What You Hear!

You can prove your thoughts wrong by shifting your focus to what is around you instead of focusing on your negative thoughts. When your thoughts start to get the better of you, try looking outside instead of listening to them inside. It is important to remain aware of what it is that is causing you anxiety so that you can rectify the situation and ultimately solve it. What you are truly looking for is awareness.

"When you can't change the situation, change your attention." -Wayne Dyer

What You Focus On Will Change!

In order to most effectively shift your focus to what's around you, it's important to pay close attention to your surroundings. It's also important to focus on what is happening around you, rather than focusing on negative thoughts that are causing you anxiety in the first place. When you look at something that causes you fear, and instead of focusing on that fear and anxiety — instead find something else. Something else that takes over your mind like a wildfire or a raging storm. Something that takes over the negative and replaces it with happiness!

Negative emotions are like fire. They burn brightly, but they burn fast. Anxious feelings can be just as powerful, except that instead of burning brightly, they linger around long after the flame has gone out. Negative feelings like anxiety and fear are temporary...they cannot last forever. By shifting your focus to positive things you can reignite the fire inside of you and enjoy a more fulfilling life!

"Everything in life is temporary....whether it is a good or bad situation. That is why you should be prepared." -Wayne Dyer

Manage Your Thoughts: It's All About the Thinking!

In order to control your anxious feelings and to better understand the thoughts that cause you anxiety, it's important to learn how to manage your thoughts. If you can't think positively, how will you ever manage your anxiety? One of the most successful ways I've heard of was described by... wait for it...Wayne Dyer in his book: "Life's Most Important Lesson". This quote explains why it's so important to focus on the positive: "...life doesn't have a lot of positive moments or good things happening all the time. But then one day something really good does happen. And when it does, you have to notice it. You have to appreciate it. Because those moments are few and far between."

If you cannot find the good in a situation or around you, your anxiety will only get worse. This is why it's so important that you start to shift your focus away from what is causing your anxiety and towards what makes you feel happy! I love the quote above because it reminds us that life isn't all about being happy all of the time. It teaches us that when one of those "few and far between" positive moments arise, we must absolutely enjoy them! We must be aware of them. We must appreciate them. Because if we're not, we miss the opportunity to enjoy them!

Everything around us is temporary...whether it is a good or bad situation. That is why you should be prepared with the tools that will allow you to manage your thoughts and emotions. If you can't control your thoughts, it will be very hard for you to control your anxiety!

"The nature of things has always been and will always be change." -Wayne Dyer

You Can't Stop Change!

Change isn't something that can be stopped. We can try our best to stop it or try and stop living in today's world...but it's impossible. We can sit on the sidelines or do whatever we want, but change will always be there. Our job is to learn how to live with it and enjoy life while it lasts! The key to living a better life with less anxiety is to stop denying what is happening around us...and start giving life your full attention! This will allow you to manage your thoughts and feelings better...which is one of the best ways that you'll ever control your anxiety!

"You are not what you have, but what you do." -Wayne Dyer

Stop Thinking about Your Anxiety Problems

It's important that we stop thinking about our anxiety because it never helps us get rid of our anxiety. In fact, it will only make our anxiety worse. It's essential that you learn to take control of your thoughts. Start by trying to stop thinking about your anxiety and start thinking about something else instead!

"If you want to get rid of anxiety, keep worrying." -Anaïs Nin

Problem Solving: The Best Way to Control Your Anxiety

In order to solve a problem, we first have to identify it. What is causing you anxiety? What are the negative thoughts that are causing your anxiety? If we can effectively identify where our negative thoughts come from, then we can start deciding whether they're valid or not. We start to realize that some of our thoughts are invalid. And if they're invalid, then we have to learn how to ignore them!

"Most of our fears are tissue paper tigers. They never roar, and if we see them clearly, they turn and run." -Wayne Dyer

No Matter what happens...You'll Be Okay!

The point is that no matter what happens you'll be okay! You'll be okay even after a loss. Even after a failure. Even after a setback or a disappointment...you will still be okay! There is an infinite number of possibilities for you in life. But every possibility has one thing in common: TIME. Every possibility is subject to time and it's impossible to predict how much time you have...or what tomorrow might bring.

"The word 'crisis' is often used by people to refer to the most complicated problems they have." -Wayne Dyer

Don't Think Too Much, Just Be

Thinking too much about your problems is one of the biggest risks you can take in life. It's a risk that we often take without realizing it! We all tend to overthink everything and allow our minds to run wild. Before we know it, we're intimidated by our own thoughts because we're thinking too far ahead into the future. But we've got to stop thinking for a little while and go back to being! We need to break out of our own heads and once again feel the natural order of things. We need to feel the order of life in our lives. And when we do, we'll know how to manage yourthoughts.

"Try not to become a man of success, but rather try to become a man of value." -Albert Einstein

Figure Out What Makes You Feel Good

The more you realize what makes you feel good, the happier you'll be. The more comfortable you are with yourself...the freer you will be. Do what makes you happy now!

Stop thinking about anxiety...forget about it! Since we're all different, it's important that you ask yourself what makes you feel good. Is it writing? Painting? Dancing? Singing? Playing the guitar? Playing baseball? Playing basketball or football? It doesn't matter what you do...as long as it makes you feel good!

"I think the best way to find yourself is to lose yourself in the service of others." -Ralph Waldo Emerson

Be Happy Right Now...For the Rest of Your Life

Our main goal in life is to be happy. But if we can't manage our anxiety, we'll never be happy. This is because anxiety causes such a lot of stress that we can't really enjoy life. We can't enjoy life because the way our mind is working right now, we're constantly thinking of all of the ways we could die. We're constantly thinking about all of the situations that we fear could happen in the future...and how they could cause us harm. All of these thoughts are causing us stress. Stress causes fear and fear causes stress!

"We become what we think about." -Earl Nightingale

Putting Your Mind in the Present

You have to shift your focus away from your anxiety and onto something else... something that you can feel right here and now! You have to think positively. Think about the things you like and enjoy. Think about all of the good things in your life. Be positive because if you're positive, then your brain will shift into autopilot! Your mind won't run wild with negative thoughts anymore. You'll be able to enjoy your life...and be happy...right now!

No More Denying

Denial is another great way that we keep our anxiety running in our lives. Denial might be the best way to overcome our anxiety. In a way, denial allows us to control our lives and give our lives a purpose! Denial prevents us from believing that we have any problems. So it's important that we get rid of this bad habit once and for all. But how do we do that? We need to first recognize denial in ourselves so that we can ignore it!

"Our true destiny is not merely to be free, but free to fail." -Samuel Beckett

Believe In Yourself

Having faith in yourself is one of the best things you can do in life! Your mind will start running wild with negative thoughts when you doubt yourself…and that's never good. But if you try to change your thinking, your mind will think of all of the reasons why you can't accomplish something. The poor thinking doesn't help you move forward either!

"The limit of my courage and confidence is the limit of my possibilities." -Albert Einstein

Get To Know Yourself Better

It's important to get to know yourself better so that you can understand what makes you happy. What makes your heart race? What kinds of things do you like to do? It's essential that we make a list or write about these things in our journals. We want to write about our passions so that we put our minds on autopilot. Think about all of your favorite things…all of the things that make you happy. If you can put these things in order, you'll know where to start first!

"Put your heart, mind, and soul into even your smallest acts. This is the secret of success." Swami Sivananda

Stop Thinking in Black or White Terms

Life isn't good or bad...it's more like a range of grey in between. Every experience we have is simply an experience. They are not either good or bad but a combination of both. We must stop thinking in black or white terms and start looking at the bigger picture. We need to step back and look at the other side of the coin sometimes so that we can see more clearly!

"When you change the way you look at things, the things you look at change." -Wayne Dyer

Change Your Perspective

We need to remember that we all have our own perspectives on life. And it's always a good idea to step back from time to time...and think about this perspective. This way, we can think about our thoughts in a better way. We'll be able to look at our problems more rationally and logically because we're not caught up in our thoughts. By watching our own brain working, we can figure out what makes us feel good...and what makes us feel bad!

"For me, growing older is a continuous learning process which I enjoy immensely." -Shirley MacLaine

Learn From Your Mistakes

We all make mistakes from time to time. It's a natural part of life. We shouldn't beat ourselves up when we make a mistake. This will only cause more problems in our lives. Instead, we should learn from our mistakes. We should try to figure out what caused the mistake and how we can fix it so it doesn't happen again!

"Life is like riding a bicycle. To keep your balance, you must keep moving." -Albert Einstein

Learn From Your Failures

Example: You have something that you want to accomplish in life and you work really hard towards it but you fail. This is not necessarily a bad thing because you'll be able to go back and see what didn't work...and how you can make it work next time. Make a list of things you've tried in the past and cross them off one by one until you're left with only one thing to do. This way, you'll know what to do!

"You miss 100% of the shots you don't take." Wayne Gretzky

Let Go Of The Past

We have to let go of the past if we ever want to have a good future. It's important that we stop living in the past and get rid of all of the negative things in our lives! Being present is essential. We need to be here now...in order for our minds to focus on what's important.

"People sometimes say that motivation doesn't last. Well, neither does bathing - that's why we recommend it daily." -Zig Ziglar

Don't Worry

Worrying about things that might go wrong in the future is a waste of time. Whenever we worry about something, two things happen. First, our minds start running wild with negative thoughts. Secondly, the stress we're feeling starts to paralyze us! The best way to overcome worry is to recognize it and then get rid of it immediately! The more time we spend worrying about something...the worse off we'll be!

"Do not dwell in the past, do not dream of the future, concentrate the mind on the present moment. This is the key to happiness." Buddha

Stop Worrying About the Future

Example: You have the intention of doing something in your future but you think a lot about it. As you're thinking about it, nervousness fills your body. This is good! Sometimes if we stop worrying about the future, our mind will wander inwards and we'll become present. In order to accomplish our goals...we must be focused on now and not worry!

"You cannot climb a mountain until you are ready to sit still and wait for hours. You cannot learn to become rich without first waiting for weeks or even months for a paycheck." Robert Kiyosaki

Stop Worrying About The Past

Example: You have something that happened in the past that you can't do anything about. So use it as an experience. It's a really great opportunity to learn from it and move forward with your life! We must stop worrying about what has happened to us in the past...and concentrate on what we're doing right now! Remember, this will help us to be present. Being present allows us to accomplish our goals!

Be Present

"Life is like photography. You use the negatives to develop. But it is better to develop once and have few negatives than to be taken by them all. -Charles Bukowski

"People sometimes say that motivation doesn't last. Well, neither does bathing - that's why we recommend it daily. The way to be motivated is to make a list of the reasons you are going to do it, and then check them off one by one." -Zig Ziglar

"Life is like photography. You use the negatives to develop. But it is better to develop once and have few negatives than to be taken by them all." -Charles Bukowski Stop Worrying About the Present

"You cannot climb a mountain until you are ready to sit still and wait for hours. You cannot learn to become rich without first waiting for weeks or even months for a paycheck. -Robert

Conclusion

You might have anxiety-- and that's okay. Remember, there are so many great things about having this mental health disorder. And the best part is that there are always ways to better cope with it. Now go live your life.

Anxiety is a mental health disorder characterized by excessive worry and generalized fear, often to the point of panic attacks and paranoia. Anxiety disorders are the most common mental illness in America; millions experience it at some point in their lives, but only around 40% seek treatment for it due to embarrassment or lack of access.

Here are some common anxieties that people experience, along with ways to deal with them.

It's important to remember that oftentimes, anxiety can be a normal emotional response. For example: you may feel anxious when speaking in public, but the anxiety often passes as soon as the speech is over. Similarly, it's not uncommon for someone to experience anxiety during a test or exam-- and that anxiety may get worse after the test has ended.

On the other hand, over time, if your anxieties are constant and persistent-- if they don't subside on their own-- you should consider seeing a mental health professional such as a psychiatrist, therapist or psychologist. Here are some common anxieties-- and what you can do about them.

Test Anxiety

Test anxiety is tough to deal with, and it can cause a lot of stress in all aspects of your life. If you have this anxiety, here are some ways to deal with it:

Realize that the exam itself is not as important as you think. In other words, realize that there's a chance-- albeit small-- that you might fail the exam. Remember, failing an exam hardly means the end of your academic career- for example, many people get placed in summer school and then pass the class after re-taking it.

. In other words, realize that there's a chance- albeit small-- that you might fail the exam. Remember, failing an exam hardly means the end of your academic career-- for example, many people get placed in summer school and then pass the class after re-taking it. To help cope with test anxiety, try not to study all day. Studies have shown that cramming can actually cause memory impairments-- so try to spread out your studying for an upcoming exam over several sessions across different days.

. Studies have shown that cramming can actually cause memory impairments-- so try to spread out your studying for an upcoming exam over several sessions across different days. Don't delay the exam until the last minute. This can lead to test anxiety.

. This can lead to test anxiety. If you're feeling particularly anxious, consider taking a regular dose of your medication before the exam-- and be sure to take it even if you don't feel any negative symptoms.

Over-Exercising

Eating disorders are typically associated with severe mental health disorders such as anorexia nervosa— but one of the most common ways that people cope with their mental health disorder is through overexercising. The problem with over-exercising is that it often leads to injury, which may lead to physical discomfort or pain.

Many people who over-exercise have stress and anxiety that they don't want to admit to themselves or anyone else. This is because many people mistakenly believe that they will be criticized for not working out enough, so they work out more than they need to in order to avoid this criticism. Other people may overexercise in an attempt to manage their anxiety, often by making themselves tired, and then feeling relieved once the activity is over. You can read more about how exercise can help with anxiety here.

If you're suffering from anxiety and struggling with over-exercising, here are some ways to get help:

Remember that no one expects you to be superhuman, especially when it comes to working out. Everyone has bad days— and all bodies need rest. The next time you find yourself trying to push your body farther than it wants to go, remember that this doesn't make you weak-- it makes you a healthy person who can listen and care for your body!

Make sure your workouts are done at the right time of day. For example, if you're exercising in the morning, do it at the end of your work day (before 12 p.m. or so), rather than in the middle while trying to survive rush hour traffic; likewise, avoid working out at night when you have more energy.

If possible, try not working out on the same days as your major exams or other stressful events (such as interviews). For example, if you have an exam on Monday, don't exercise on it-- and if you know that your interview is next Tuesday, try to schedule your workout for Monday.

Obsessive-Compulsive Disorder

If you have OCD, you may sometimes feel like something terrible might happen-- or that something has already happened. You may feel compelled to check everything over and over again in an attempt to gain reassurance. OCD is often a mental health disorder in which you continue to worry about something even after you've done something to end the worry.

If OCD is affecting your life, here are some ways to cope with it:

Stop obsessing over small details. It's very hard for people who live with OCD to take things that are "small" or "unimportant" seriously, because they can't see how something so small could have such a big impact on your life.

. It's very hard for people who live with OCD to take things that are "small" or "unimportant" seriously, because they can't see how something so small could have such a big impact on your life. Ask for help. If you've tried using CBT [Cognitive Behavioral Therapy] to help reduce your OCD symptoms and it hasn't been working, it may be time to seek some professional help.

Social Anxiety Disorder

Social anxiety disorder is extremely difficult to deal with-- and it can cause a lot of stress in all aspects of your life. If you have social anxiety, here are some strategies that you can use:

Remember that people aren't out to get you. You may feel like someone will judge you or say something wrong if a stranger says hello or asks how your day is going; but most people don't mean to offend others by asking such a question.

. You may feel like someone will judge you or say someth ng wrong if a stranger says hello or asks how your day is going; but most people don't mean to offend others by asking such a question. Take a social anxiety test. This test can give you an idea of what social situations might be difficult for you and how to approach them.

. This test can give you an idea of what social situations might be difficult for you and how to approach them. Avoid places that cause anxiety. If things become too much, consider avoiding situations that are known to cause your anxiety. This can be difficult to do because the more you avoid things that cause your anxiety, the more this may make you feel like a failure-- but if it's affecting your ability to function in your everyday life and making you feel overwhelmed and anxious, try to find a way to reduce your exposure.

. If things become too much, consider avoiding situations that are known to cause your anxiety. This can be difficult to do because the more you avoid things that cause your anxiety, the more this may make you feel like a failure- but if it's affecting your ability to function in your everyday life and making you feel overwhelmed and anxious, try to find a way to reduce your exposure. Get plenty of sleep. Sleep helps people with social anxiety to feel less anxious during situations that may cause them stress. Going to bed and waking up at the same time each day will help you set your body for sleep, which will help you feel ready for social interactions throughout the day. For many people, avoiding caffeine and other stimulants can reduce their anxiety; however, if this isn't working for you, then you may need to consider altering your diet.

. Sleep helps people with social anxiety to feel less anxious during situations that may cause them stress. Going to bed and waking up at the same time each day will help you set your body for sleep, which will help you feel ready for social interactions throughout the day. For many people, avoiding caffeine and other stimulants can reduce their anxiety; however, if this isn't working for you, then you may need to consider altering your diet. Stay in the moment. Try to focus on what is going on in the here and now.

. Try to focus on what is going on in the here and now. Get professional help if needed. Don't let your social anxiety disorder rules your life!

Get the help that you need to feel better and be able to interact with others.

Addiction

If you have an addiction, it can very difficult to set boundaries and know when to say "no" when it comes to the object of your addiction. Here are some strategies for managing your addiction:

Remember that nobody is perfect. For example, even people who live without addictions fail on a daily basis; however, the key is in making sure that you don't let this become a habit, and try to challenge yourself as much as possible.

. For example, even people who live without addictions fail on a daily basis; however, the key is in making sure that you don't let this become a habit, and try to challenge yourself as much as possible. If you want to stop an addiction but seem to be unable to find a way to do so, consider seeking professional help. This may seem like a scary step to take-- especially if you still have some feelings about your addiction-- but remember that there is help available for people who need it.

. This may seem like a scary step to take-- especially if you still have some feelings about your addiction-- but remember that there is help available for people who need it. Speak up for yourself. If you are being deceptive with yourself or the other adults in your life about your addiction, ask them to speak up about it. If you never learn that the person cares about you and would like to help you stop struggling with your addiction, then it could be too late.

. If you are being deceptive with yourself or the other adults in your life about your addiction, ask them to speak up about it. If you never learn that the person cares about you and would like to help you stop struggling with your addiction, then it could be too late. Mental illness. Although there isn't a lot of research about the relationship between mental illness and addictions, it has been found that many people with depression, anxiety, bipolar disorder, or schizophrenia abuse substances to cope with their conditions.

. Although there isn't a lot of research about the relationship between mental illness and addictions, it has been found that many people with depression, anxiety, bipolar disorder, or schizophrenia abuse substances to cope with their conditions. Addiction tests. It's important to take an addiction test before you try to stop your addiction so that you know how severe your addiction is.

. It's important to take an addiction test before you try to stop your addiction so that you know how severe your addiction is. Get a support system. The people in your life who care about you the most can be of the greatest help in deciding whether or not you should continue using a substance and how to stop it.

Alcoholism

Alcoholism is a problem that many people struggle with, especially if they don't realize that they have developed an addiction to alcohol. Since alcohol is legal and accessible almost anywhere, many people think drinking isn't a problem-- but this may not always be true! Here are some strategies for overcoming alcoholism:

Avoid places where alcohol is sold. If you find yourself struggling to resist alcohol, then try not to go into areas where you might be tempted to drink.

. If you find yourself struggling to resist alcohol, then try not to go into areas where you might be tempted to drink. Stay away from alcohol. You can't control how much alcohol others are drinking around you, but if someone offers you a drink, politely decline your offer.

. You can't control how much alcohol others are drinking around you, but if someone offers you a drink, politely decline your offer. Eat well and get plenty of sleep. Helps your body to recover from the negative effects of alcohol.

. Helps your body to recover from the negative effects of alcohol. Stay in control. Don't take a drink if you are feeling pressured to do so, and don't drink when you are alone; these are both common triggers leading to alcoholism.

. Don't take a drink if you are feeling pressured to do so, and don't drink when you are alone; these are both common triggers leading to alcoholism. Get professional help if needed. If you find yourself struggling despite all of your efforts, then consider contacting an addiction treatment facility for help finding a way out of your addiction.

. If you find yourself struggling despite all of your efforts, then consider contacting an addiction treatment facility for help finding a way out of your addiction. Reward yourself. You don't need to reward yourself with alcohol after a hard day, but it can be helpful to create some non-alcohol rewards that you can give yourself when you are in need of some encouragement.

. You don't need to reward yourself with alcohol after a hard day, but it can be helpful to create some non-alcohol rewards that you can give yourself when you are in need of some encouragement. The safest time is not all the time. Just because you are trying to end your addiction doesn't mean that it will be safe for you to drink on a regular basis; the safest time of the day is when you are sober.

. Just because you are trying to end your addiction doesn't mean that it will be safe for you to drink on a regular basis; the safest time of the day is when you are sober. Get help finding non-addictive ways of dealing with stress. If you've been using alcohol as a way to deal with your stress, then it's important for you to learn new ways of dealing with stress when necessary.

. If you've been using alcohol as a way to deal with your stress, then it's important for you to learn new ways of dealing with stress when necessary. Know when to say no. If you are offered alcohol and don't want to have a drink, then don't accept the offer.

. If you are offered alcohol and don't want to have a drink, then don't accept the offer. Learn about recovery. There is always help available for people looking for help with an addiction; these days there are many resources available online as well as in person!

Depression

Stressful situations can cause depression or make depression worse in some people. People who have a history of depression in their family, people that have had more than one depressive episode, and people that do not respond well to antidepressants are all at higher risk for developing depression during stressful situations. If you are worried about your ability to deal with stress, then consider the following strategies:

Turn off the television. Television can make you feel like you are being attacked-- or make you feel like you need to be perfect. This is a great strategy if watching television is causing your addiction.

. Television can make you feel like you are being attacked-- or make you feel like you need to be perfect. This is a great strategy if watching television is causing your addiction. Talk to someone. Talking to someone about what you are experiencing can help you cope with your situation, and a therapist might be able to recommend ways of coping with stress that are better for your lifestyle.

. Talking to someone about what you are experiencing can help you cope with your situation, and a therapist might be able to recommend ways of coping with stress that are better for your lifestyle. Try new hobbies. It's important never to feel like the way in which you have been coping is the only way in which you should cope! New hobbies can be an enjoyable and safe way for an individual to experience life without feeling like they have to always react to their surroundings through addictive behavior.

. It's important never to feel like the way in which you have been coping is the only way in which you should cope! New hobbies can be an enjoyable and safe way for an individual to experience life without feeling like they have to always react to their surroundings through addictive behavior. Exercise. Physical activity has shown to be a great strategy for dealing with stress.

. Physical activity has shown to be a great strategy for dealing with stress. Stay away from triggers. Take steps so that you don't encounter people or places that make your withdrawal symptoms worse when you are struggling with your addiction.

. Take steps so that you don't encounter people or places that make your withdrawal symptoms worse when you are struggling with your addiction. Stop drinking alcohol. When you are dealing with depression, it is important to stay away from alcohol to avoid making the situation worse. You don't need alcohol to get through the day or to feel happy in life!

. When you are dealing with depression, it is important to stay away from alcohol to avoid making the situation worse. You don't need alcohol to get through the day or to feel happy in life! Change your attitude toward your mental health. Don't think of yourself as crazy for getting depressed; instead try to think of your mood as a normal reaction people have when they are under a lot of stress. You are not crazy if you are depressed; you just have a normal human reaction to stress!

. Don't think of yourself as crazy for getting depressed; instead try to think of your mood as a normal reaction people have when they are under a lot of stress. You are not crazy if you are depressed; you just have a normal human reaction to stress! Talk about your feelings with others. You can't experience happiness without first feeling pain. Talk with others about the way in which you feel and what you go through, and they might be able to help you deal with things better!

. You can't experience happiness without first feeling pain. Talk with others about the way in which you feel and what you go through, and they might be able to help you deal with things better! Learn to use relaxation techniques. Relaxation techniques can be a great way for people to cope with stress. Some simple ways of relaxing include deep breathing, visualization, meditation, and exercise.

. Relaxation techniques can be a great way for people to cope with stress. Some simple ways of relaxing include deep breathing, visualization, meditation, and exercise. Change your perception of life. If your life is chronically stressful or seems like it will never improve-- change your perception! It's no fun living in a dark world where you expect the worst out of everything. Try to break away from this habit and have a more realistic outlook about the things around you instead!

. If your life is chronically stressful or seems like it will never improve-- change your perception! It's no fun living in a dark world where you expect the worst out of everything. Try to break away from this habit and have a more realistic outlook about the things around you instead! Be mindful. Being mindful can help you see what's going on around you and thus help cope with situations better. Being mindful means observing your mood regularly, being aware of how you feel, and making time for relaxation at least once a day.

. Being mindful can help you see what's going on around you and thus help you cope with situations better. Being mindful means observing your mood regularly, being aware of how you feel, and making time for relaxation at least once a day. Remember to relax. If you are not in a position where you actually feel like relaxing-- then try to keep in mind that it is important to relax from time to time! Relaxation is essential when dealing with the stress of all kinds, and it could be the first step toward finally feeling better about your life!

These are just a few suggestions for coping with depression while under the influence of drugs or alcohol. Remember that these tips are only suggestions, and what works for one person might not work as well for another! It is important to learn which strategies you can implement during your life in order to help deal with depression.

And remember: there is no shame in experiencing depression at all! You are not weak and you are not doing anything wrong by experiencing feelings of sadness and hopelessness. Depression can sometimes be an unavoidable part of life, but it doesn't have to hold you back from being happy. You are capable of overcoming your depression and moving on with your life!

www.ingramcontent.com/pod-product-compliance
Lightning Source LLC
Chambersburg PA
CBHW070911080526
44589CB00013B/1264